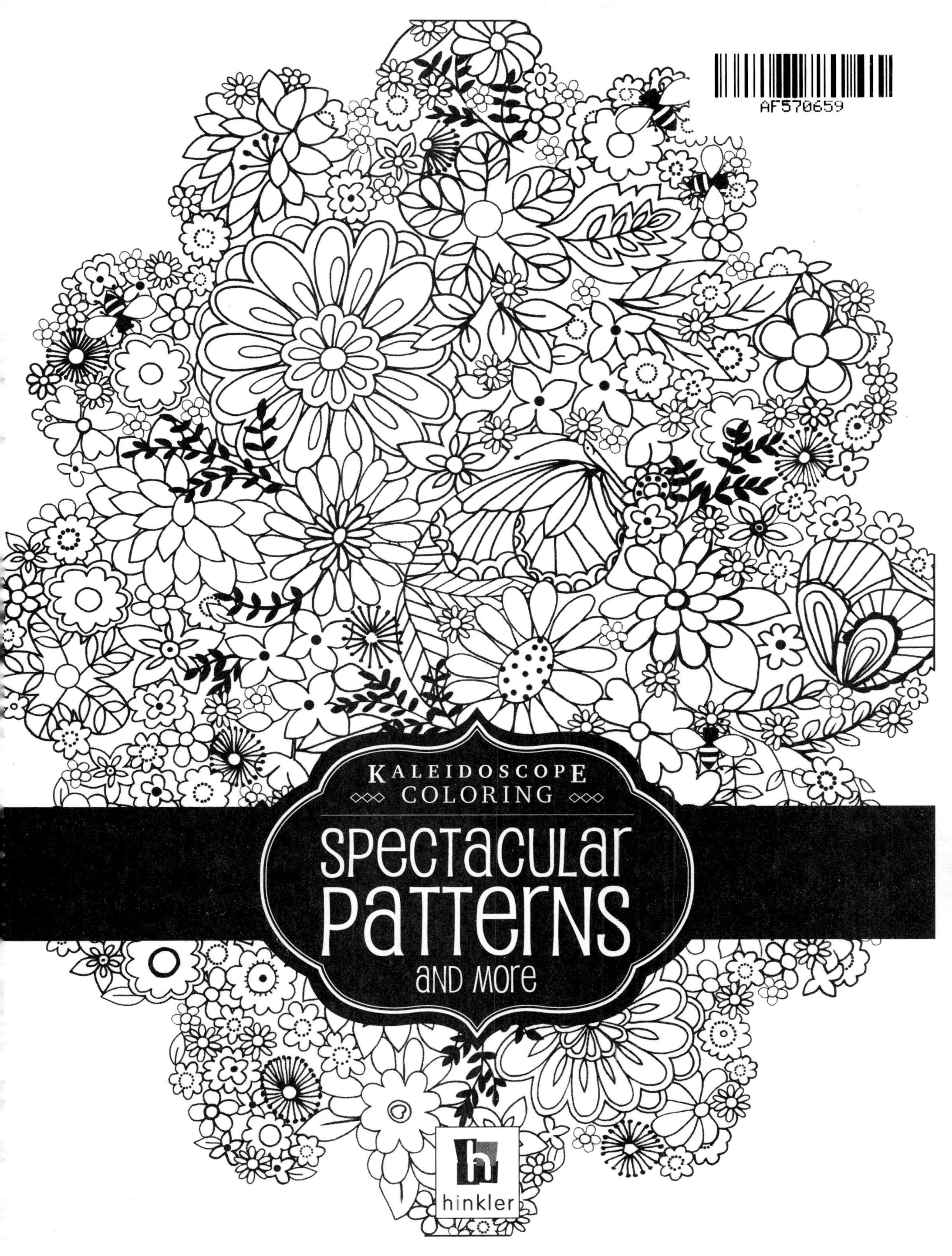
AF570659
KALEIDOSCOPE
COLORING
SPECTACULAR
PATTERNS
AND MORE
hinkler

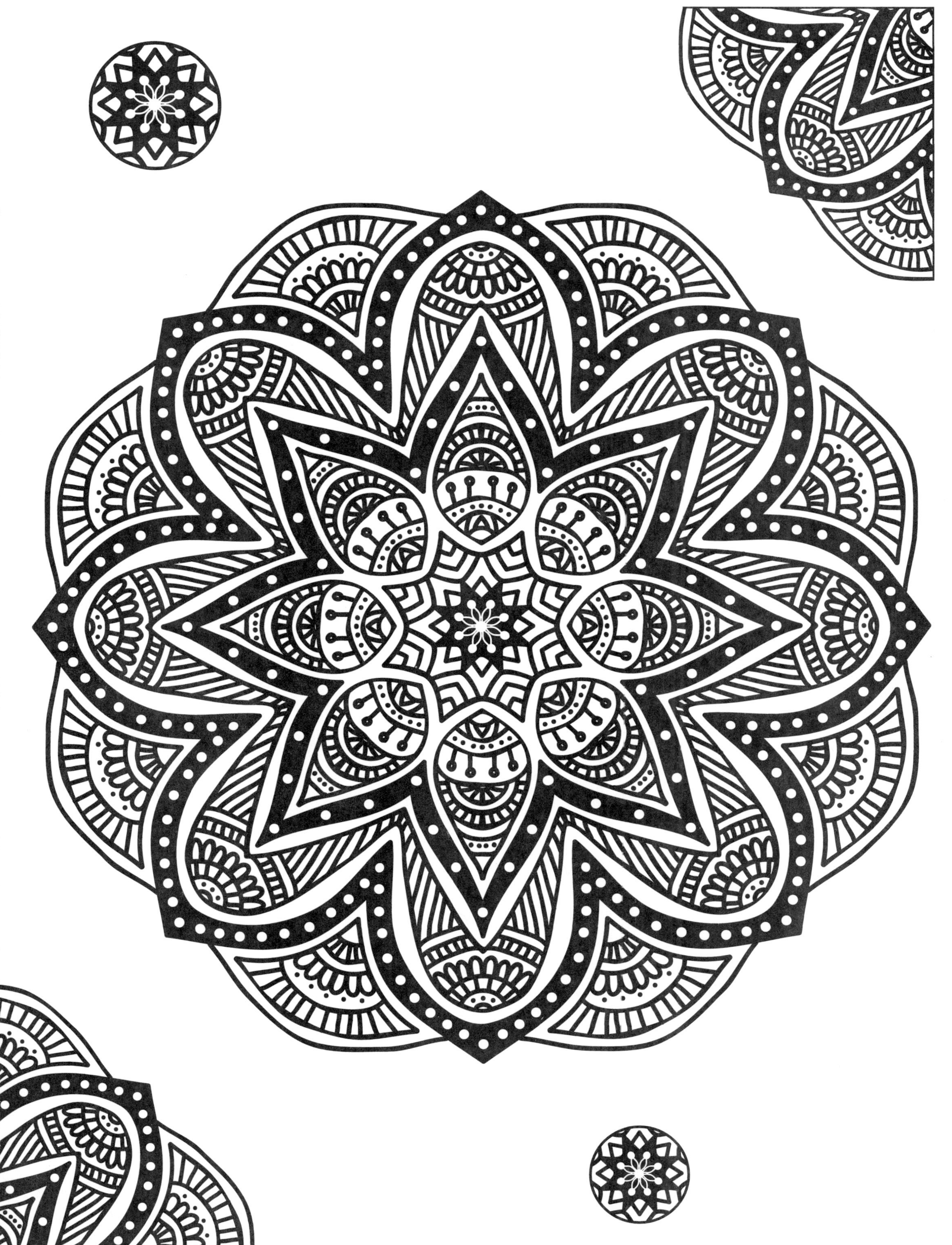

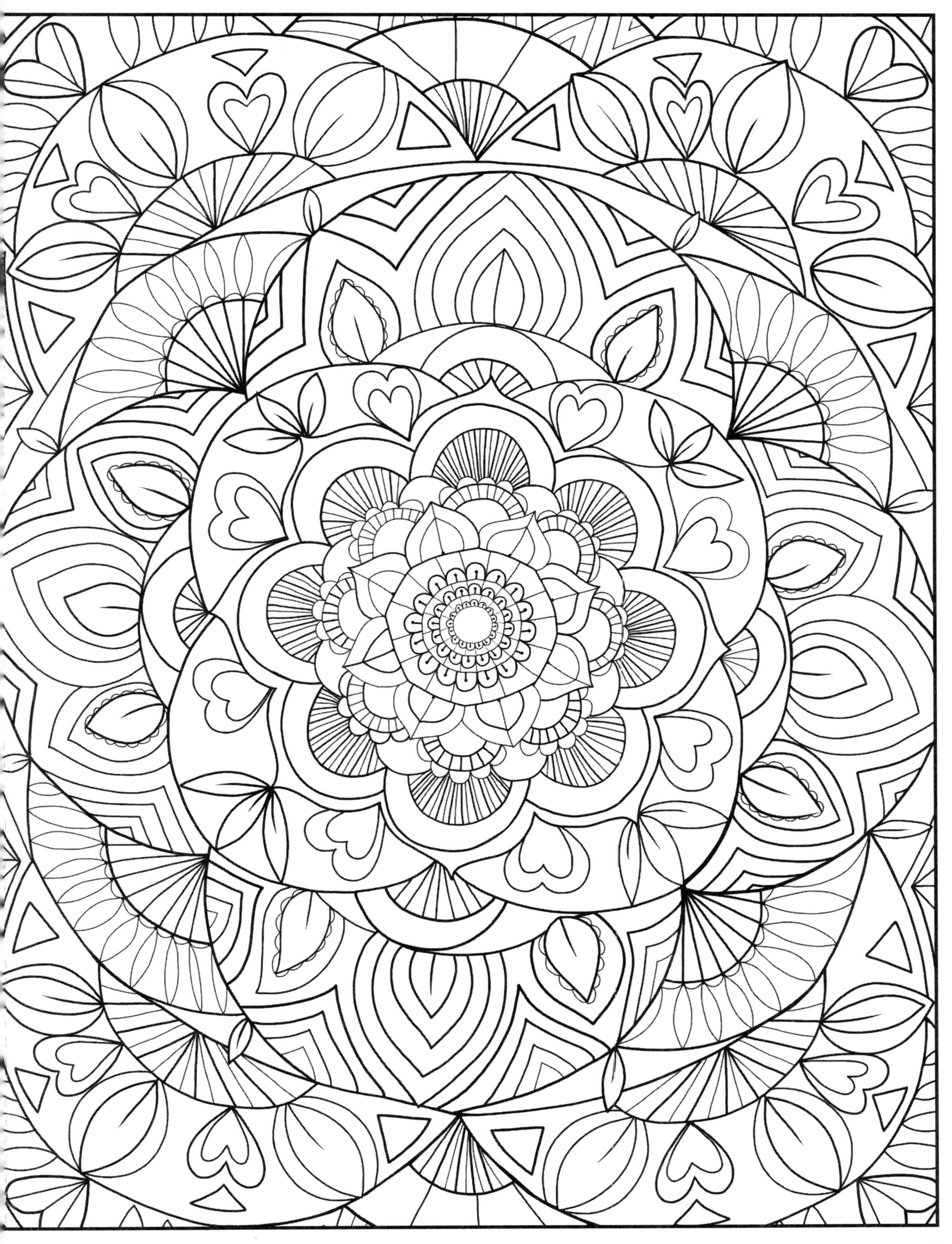

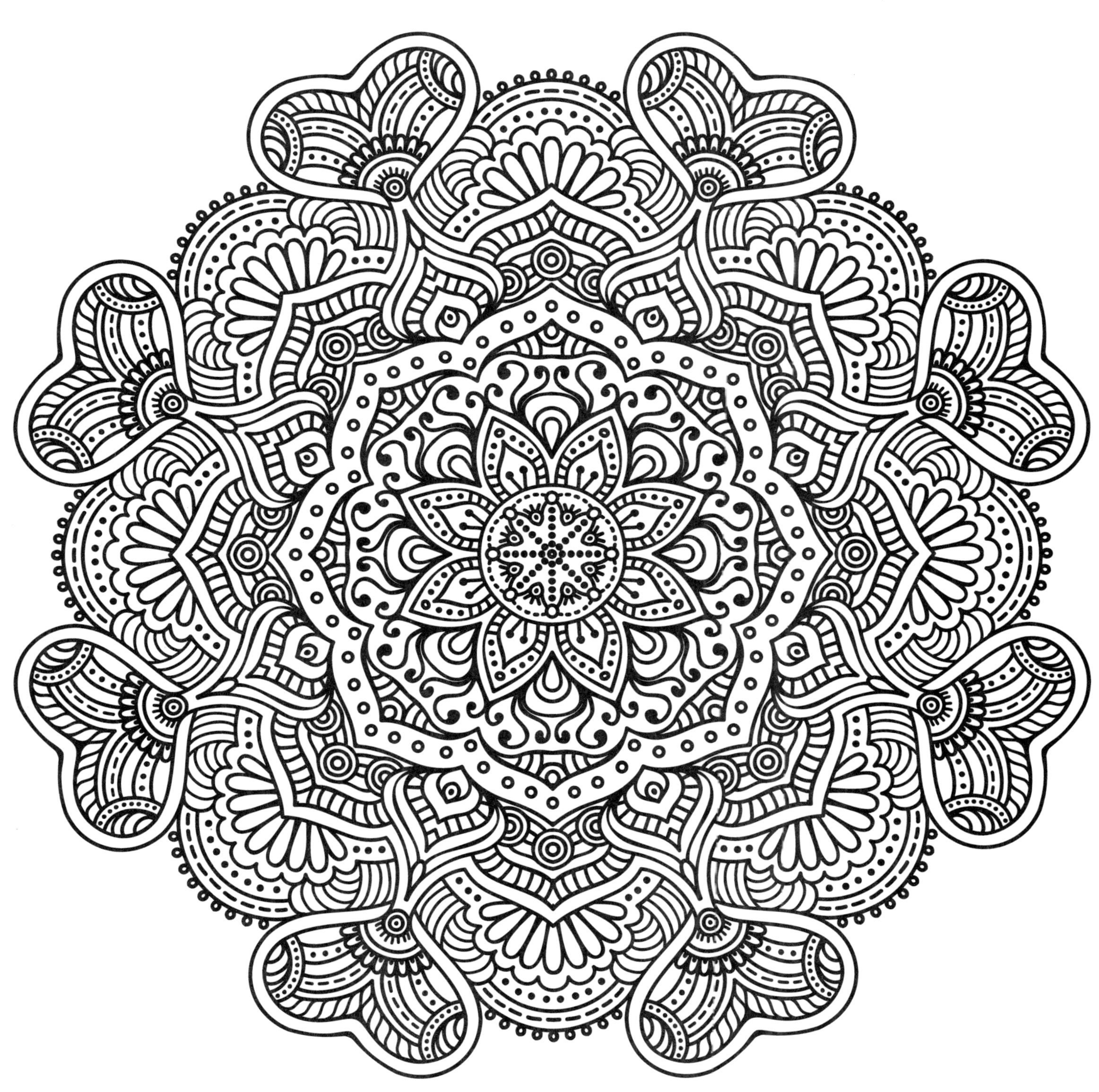

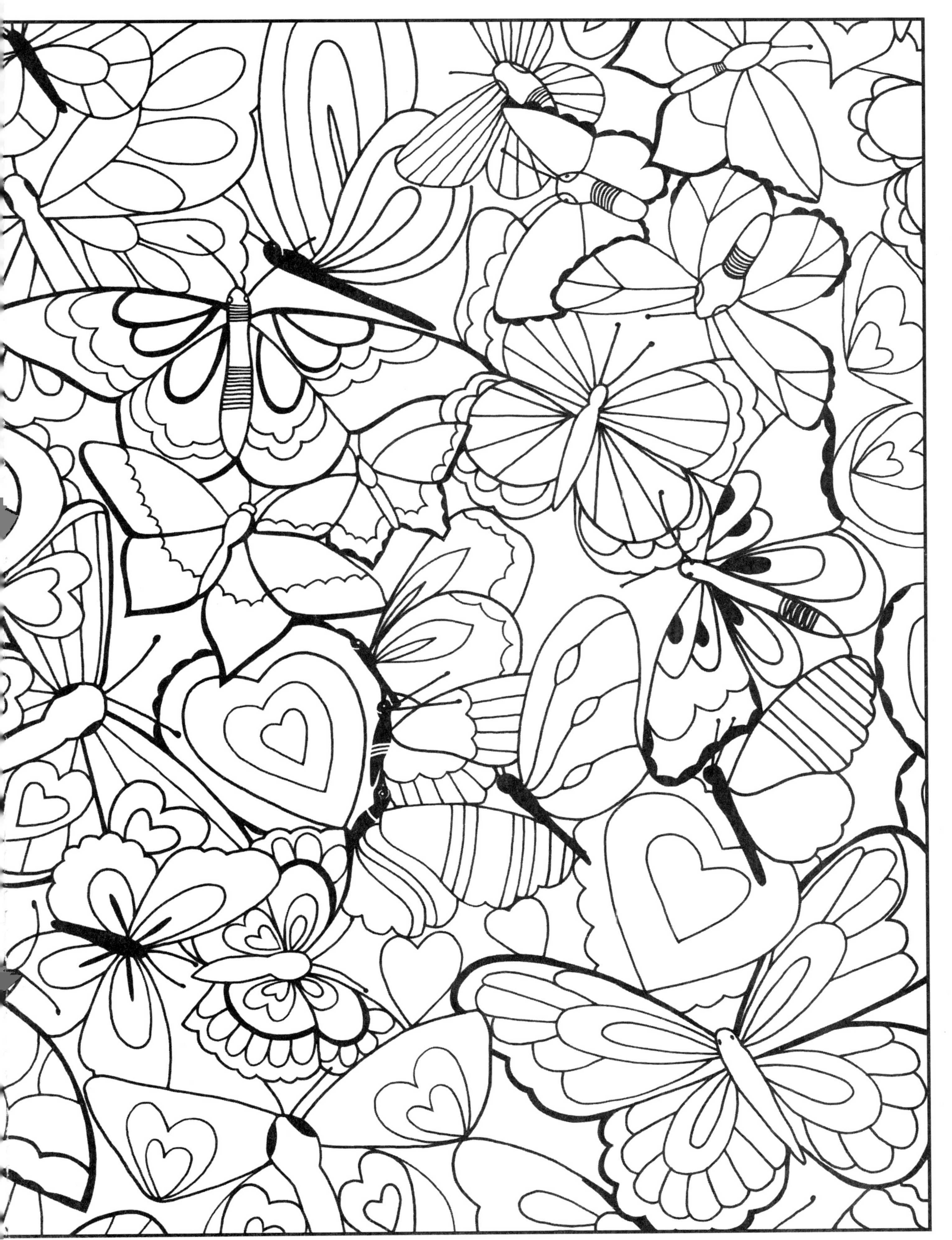

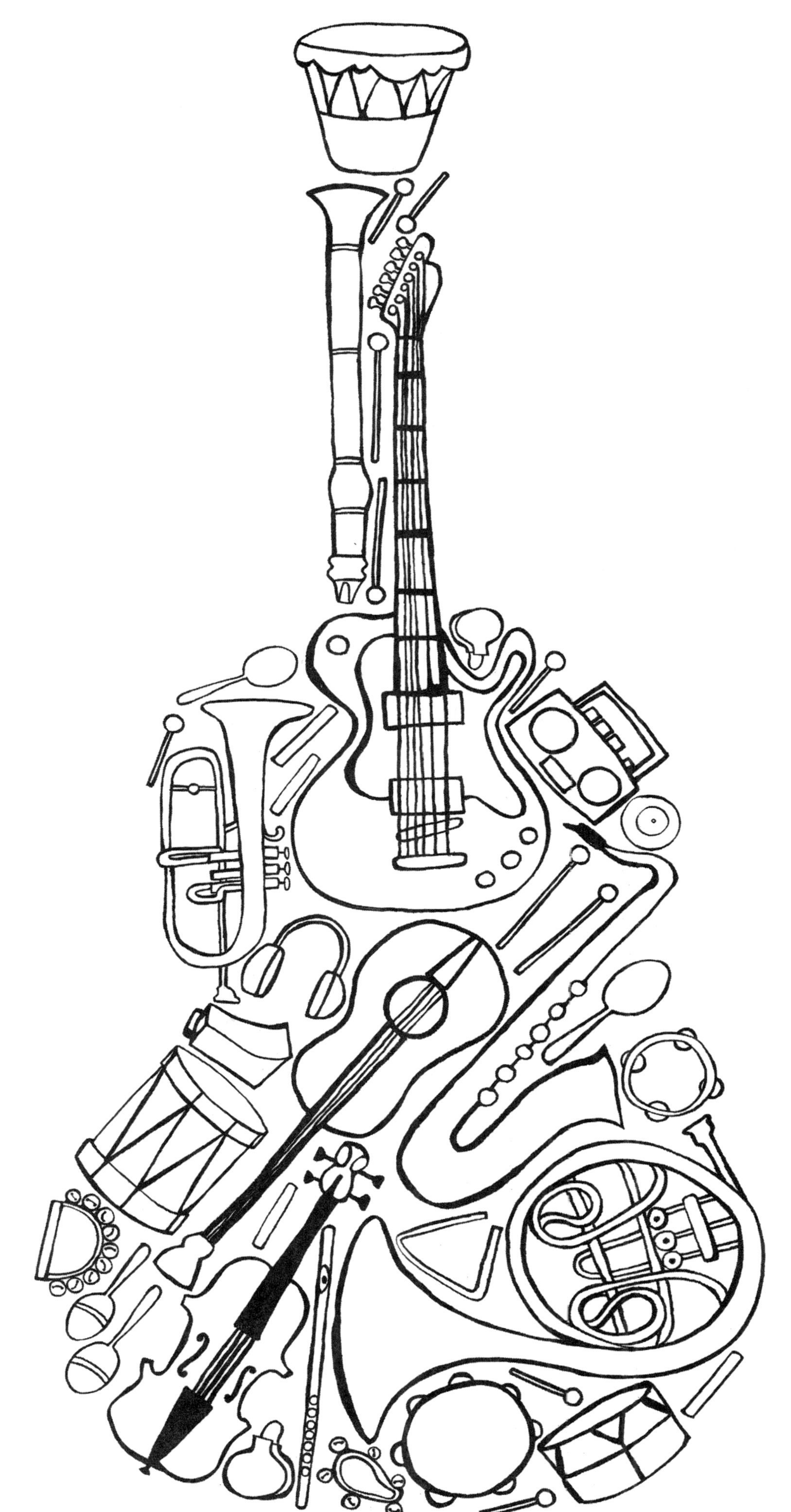

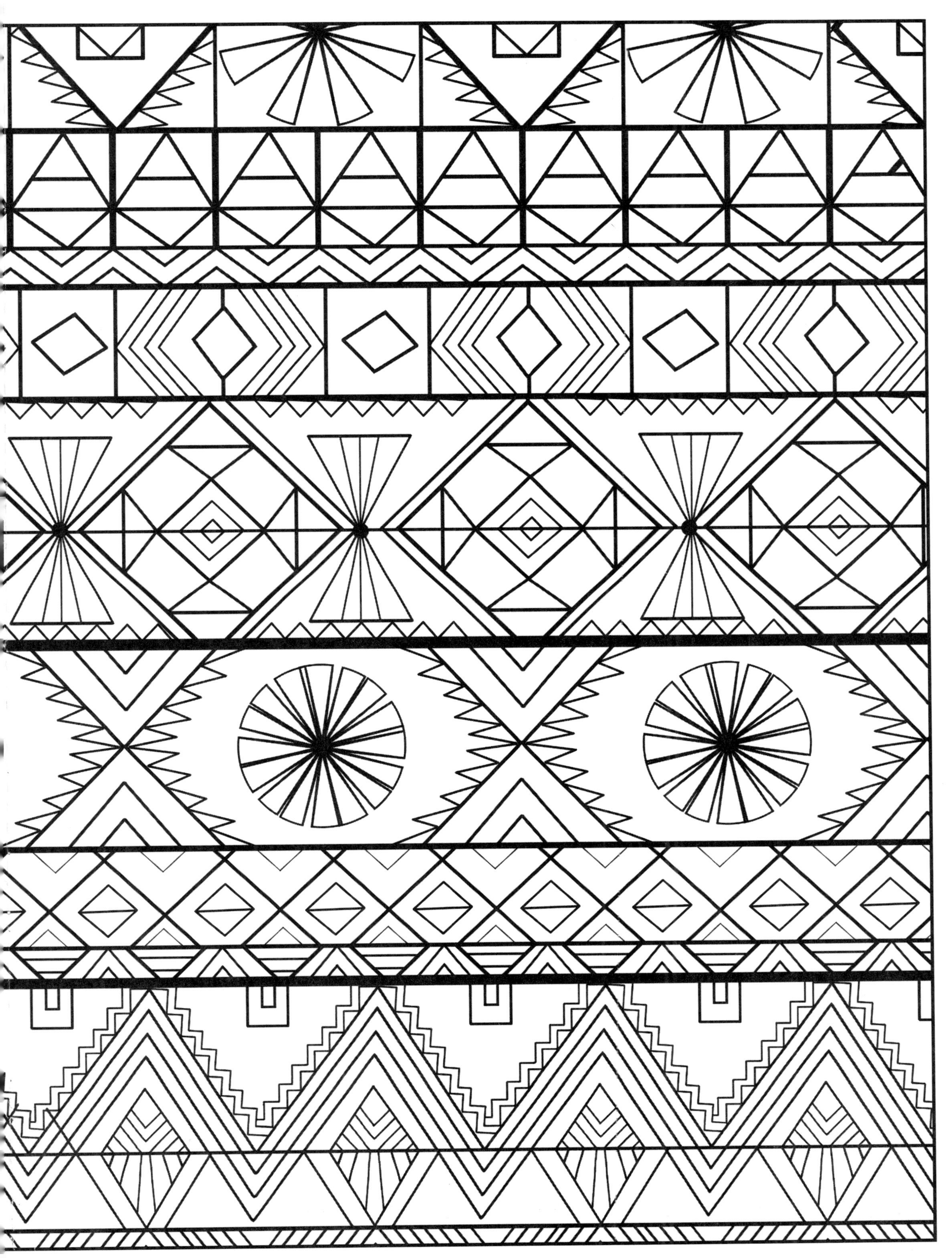

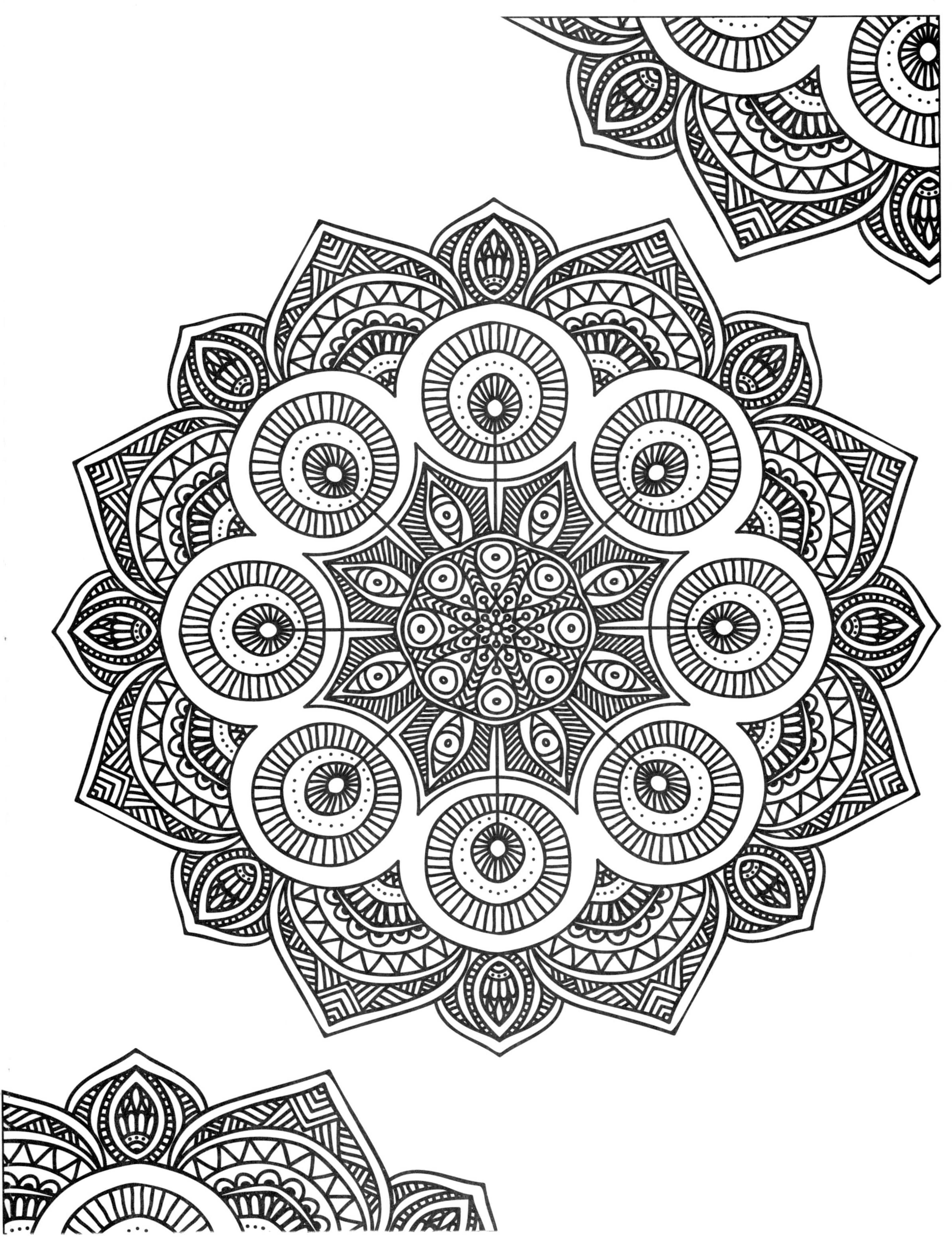

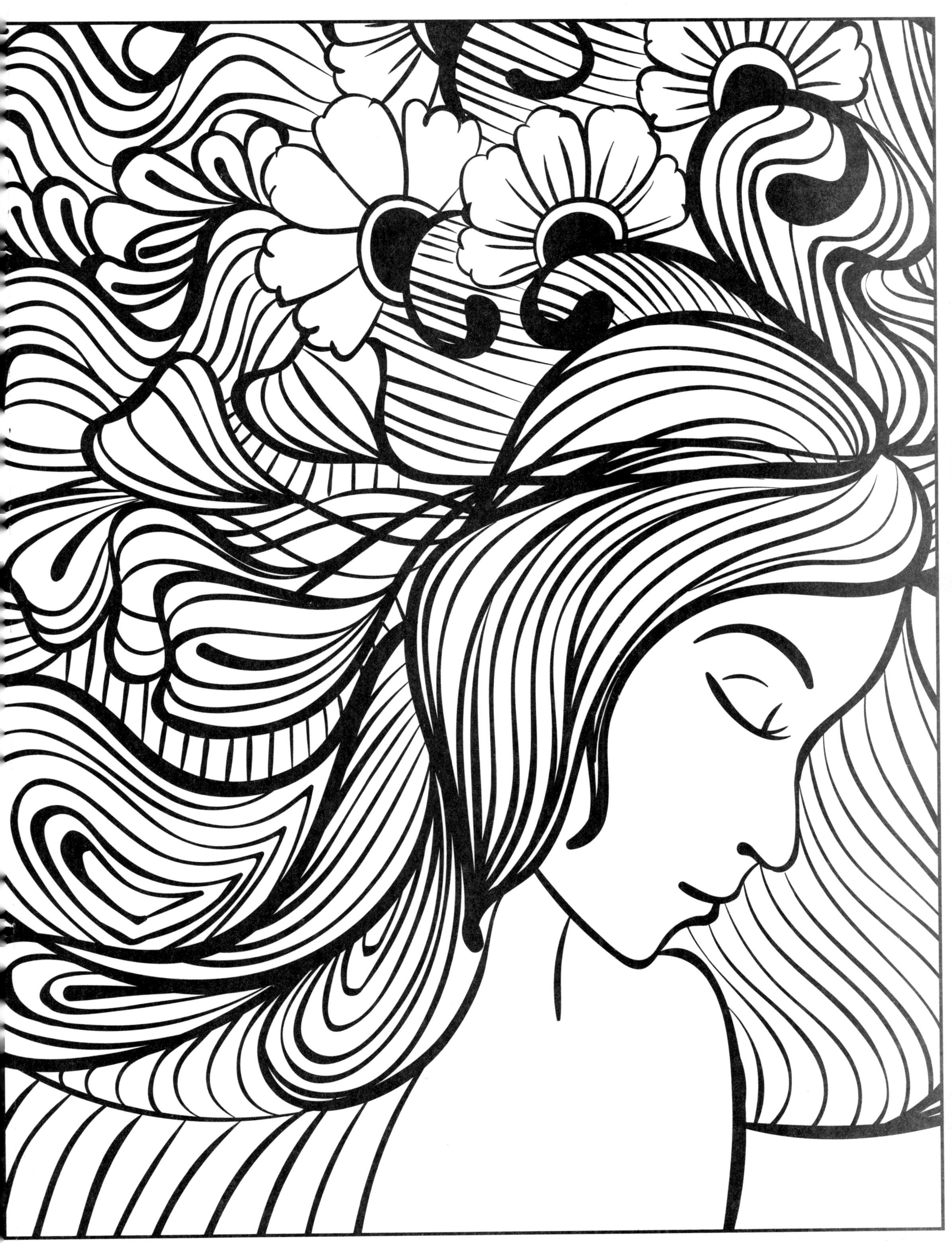

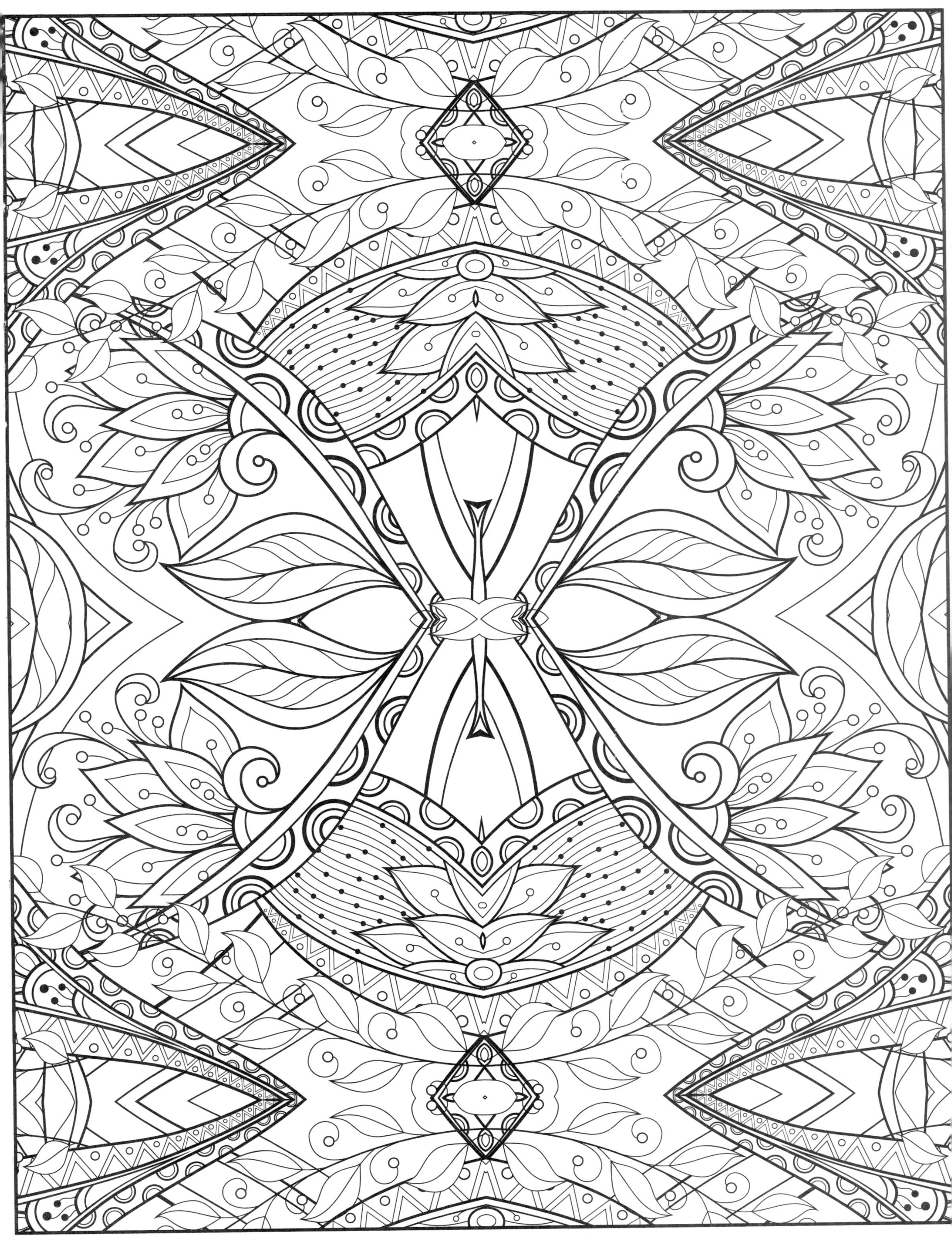

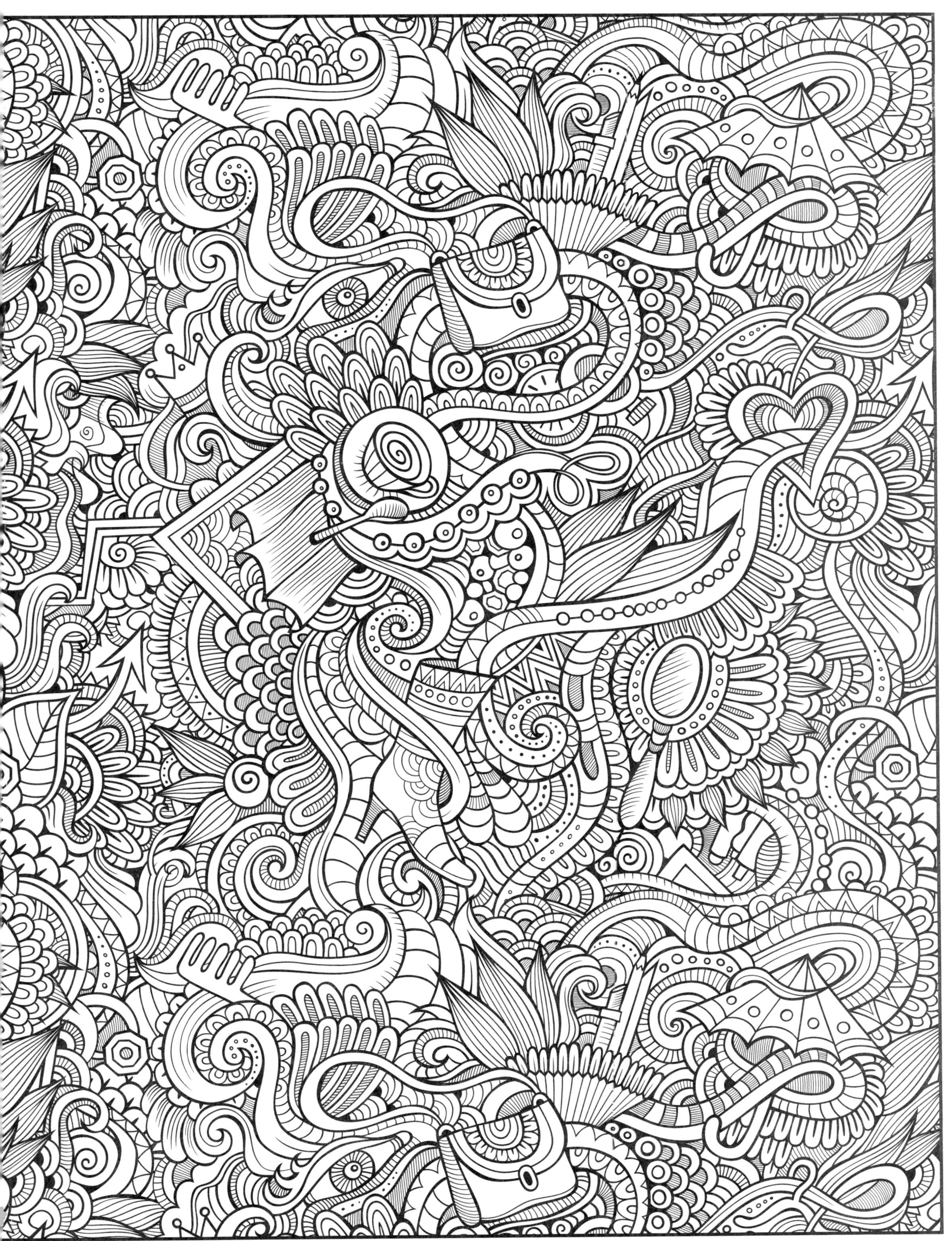

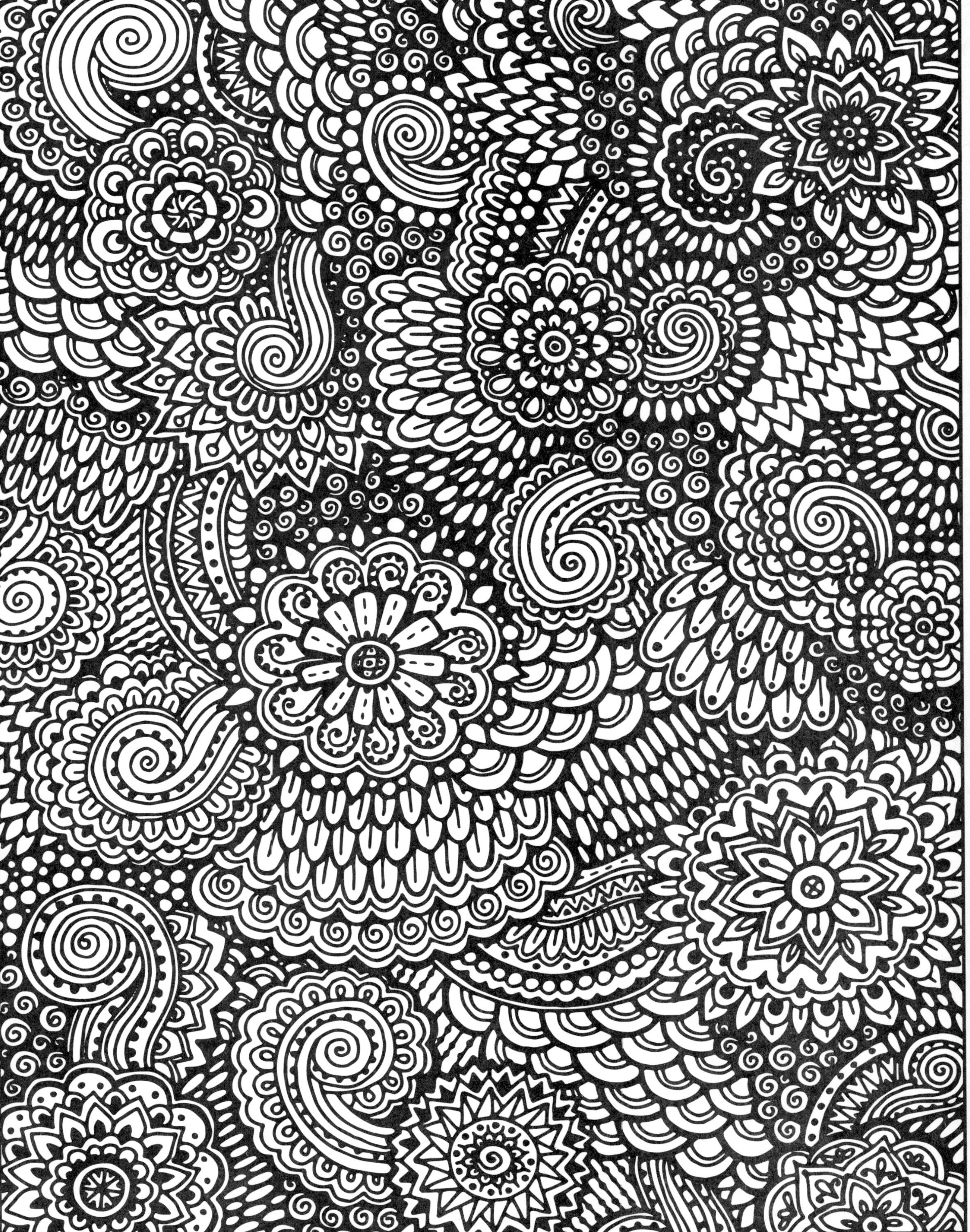

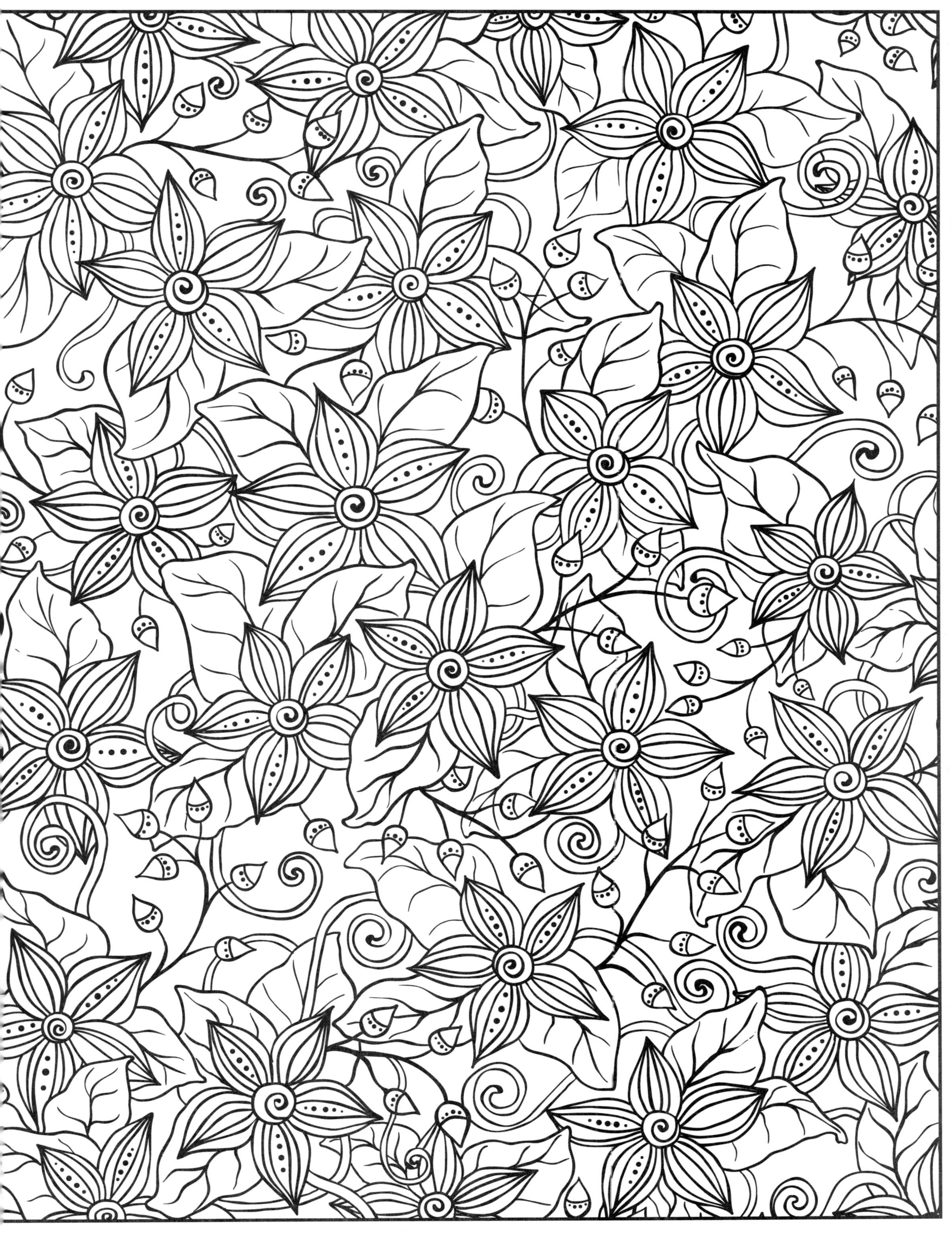

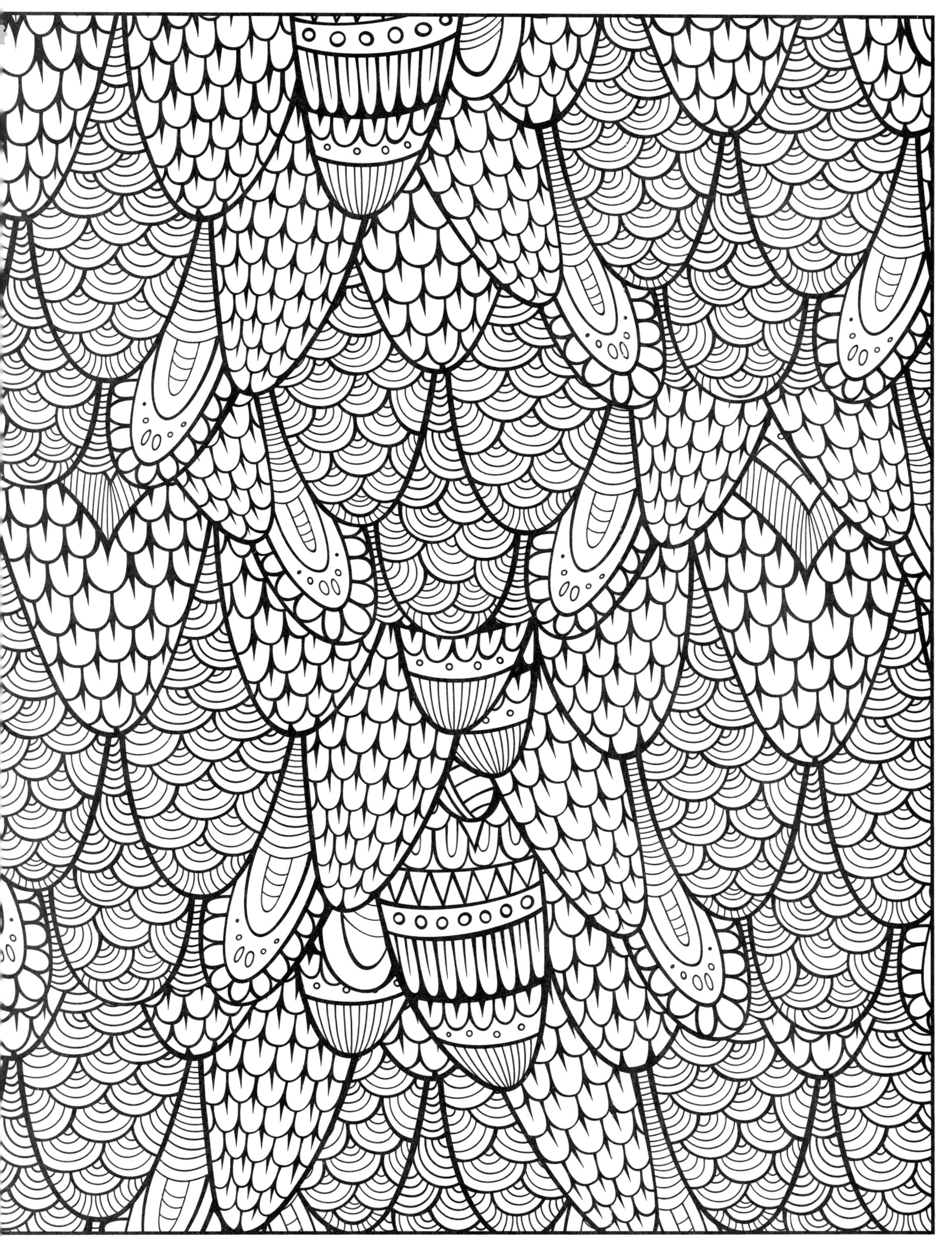

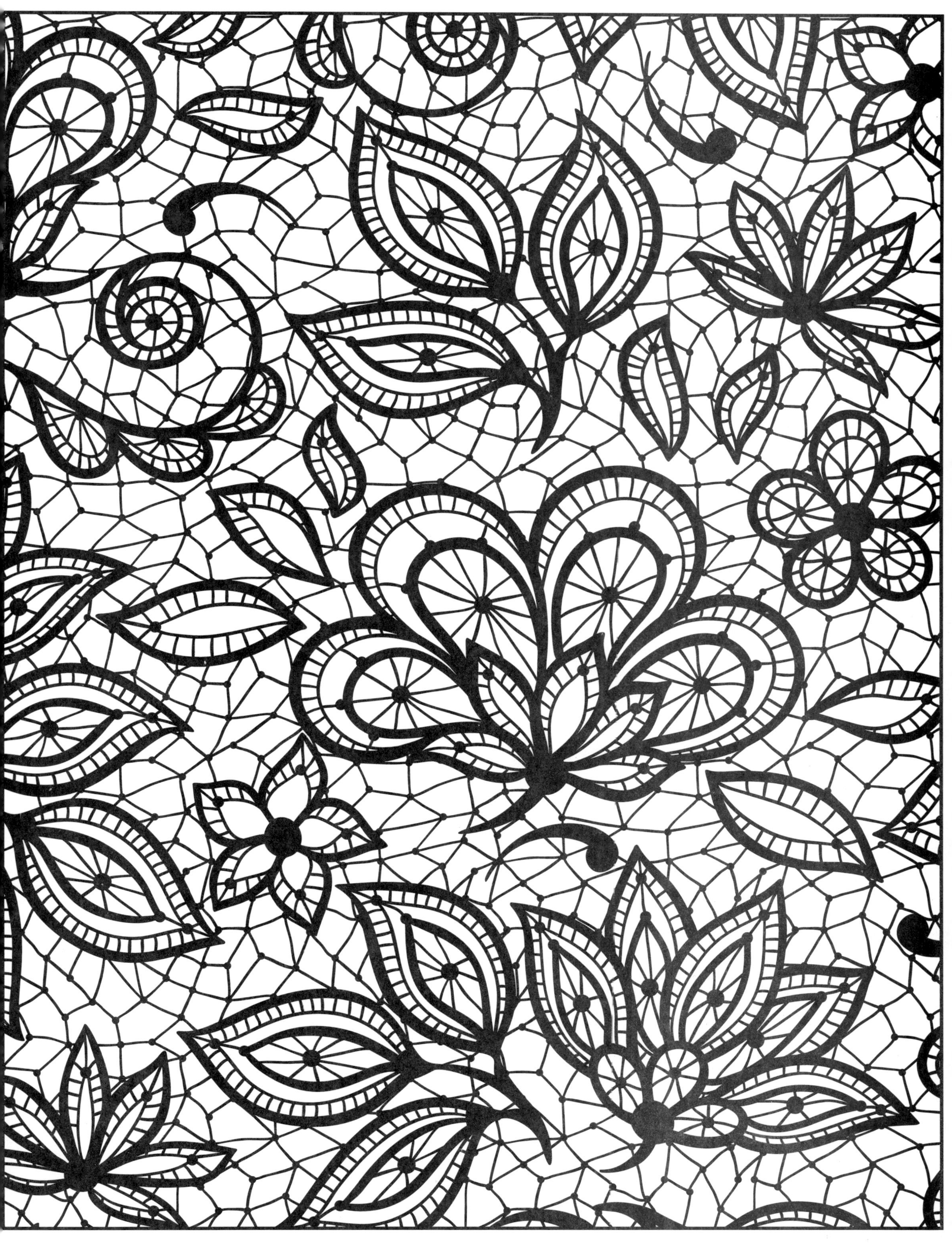

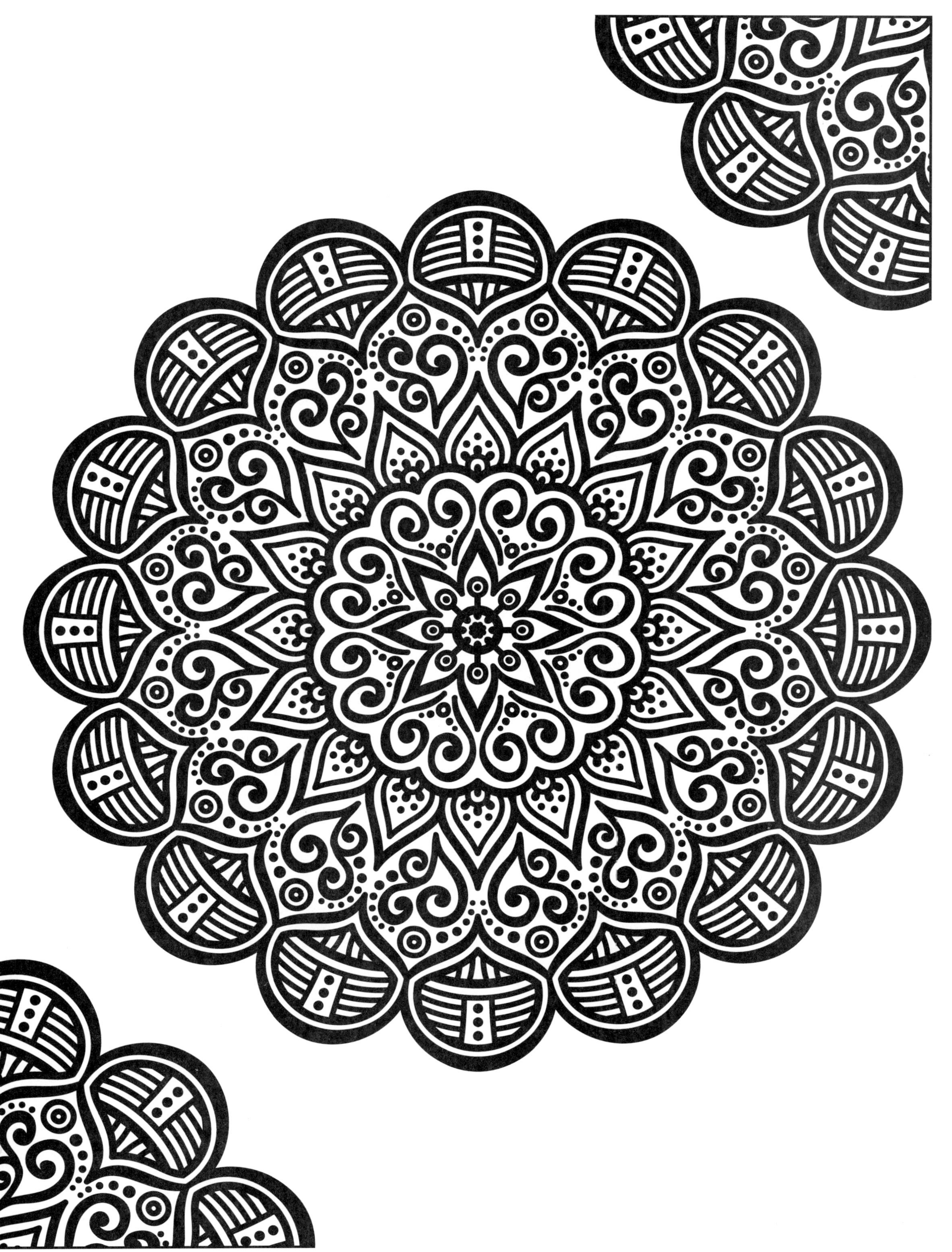

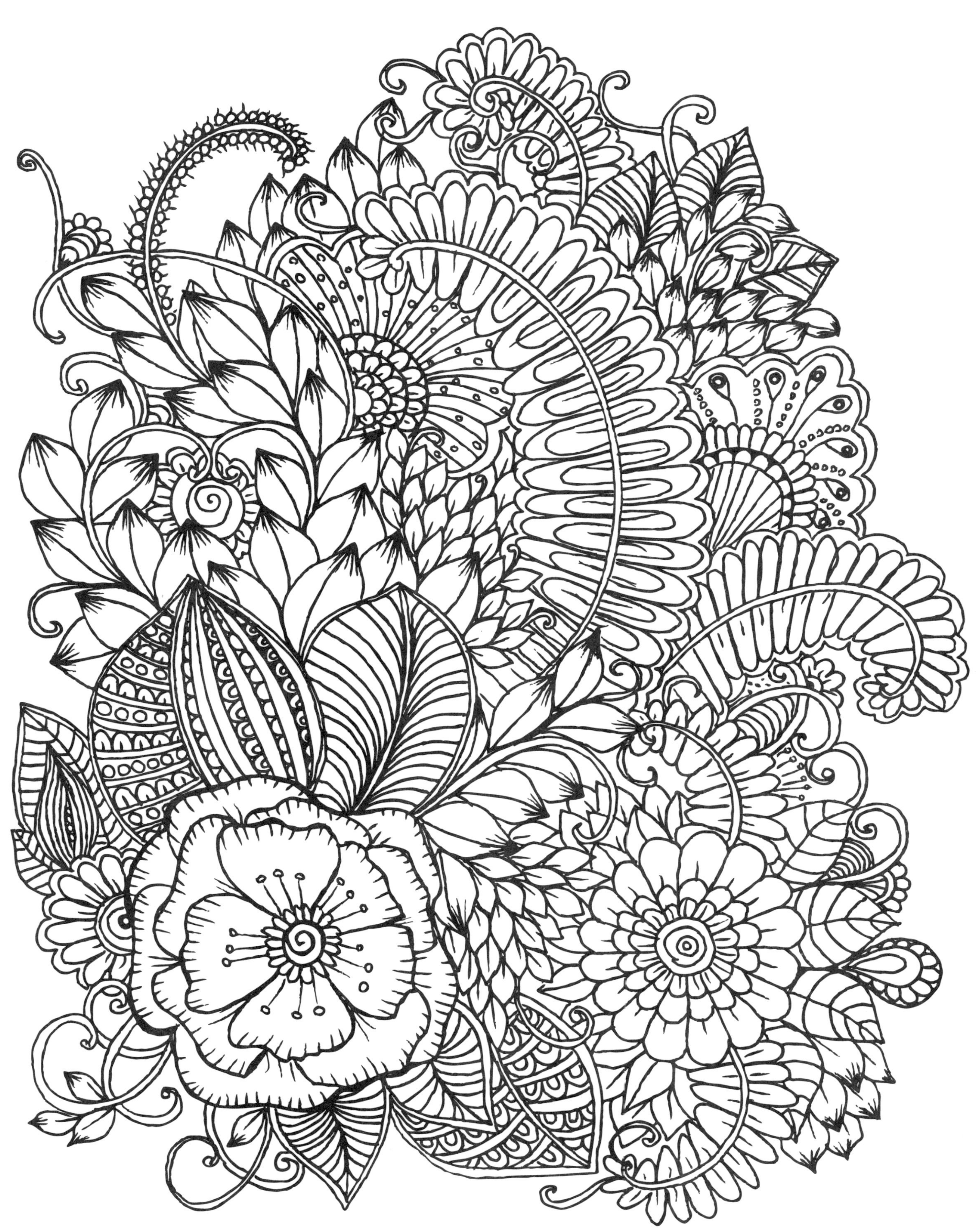

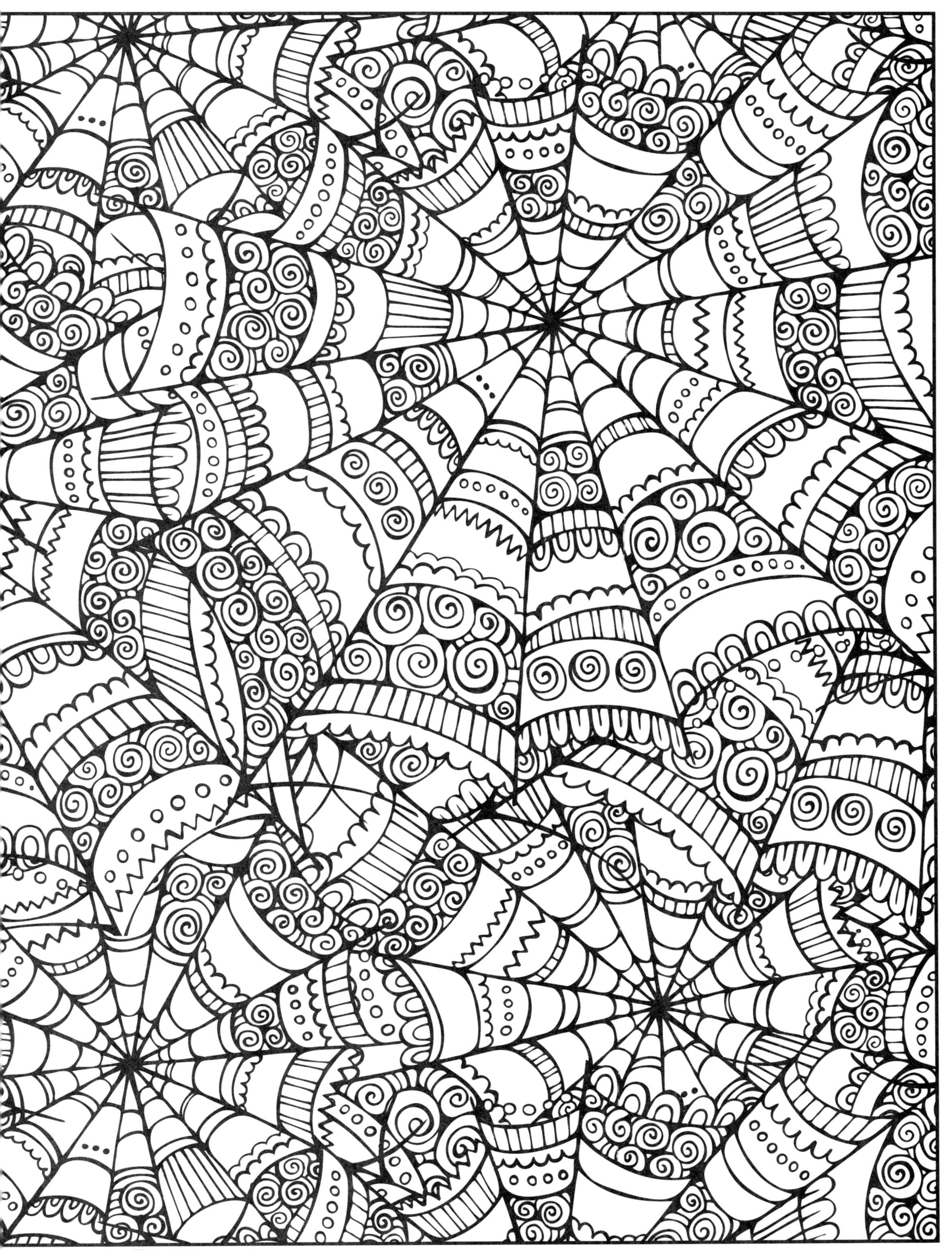

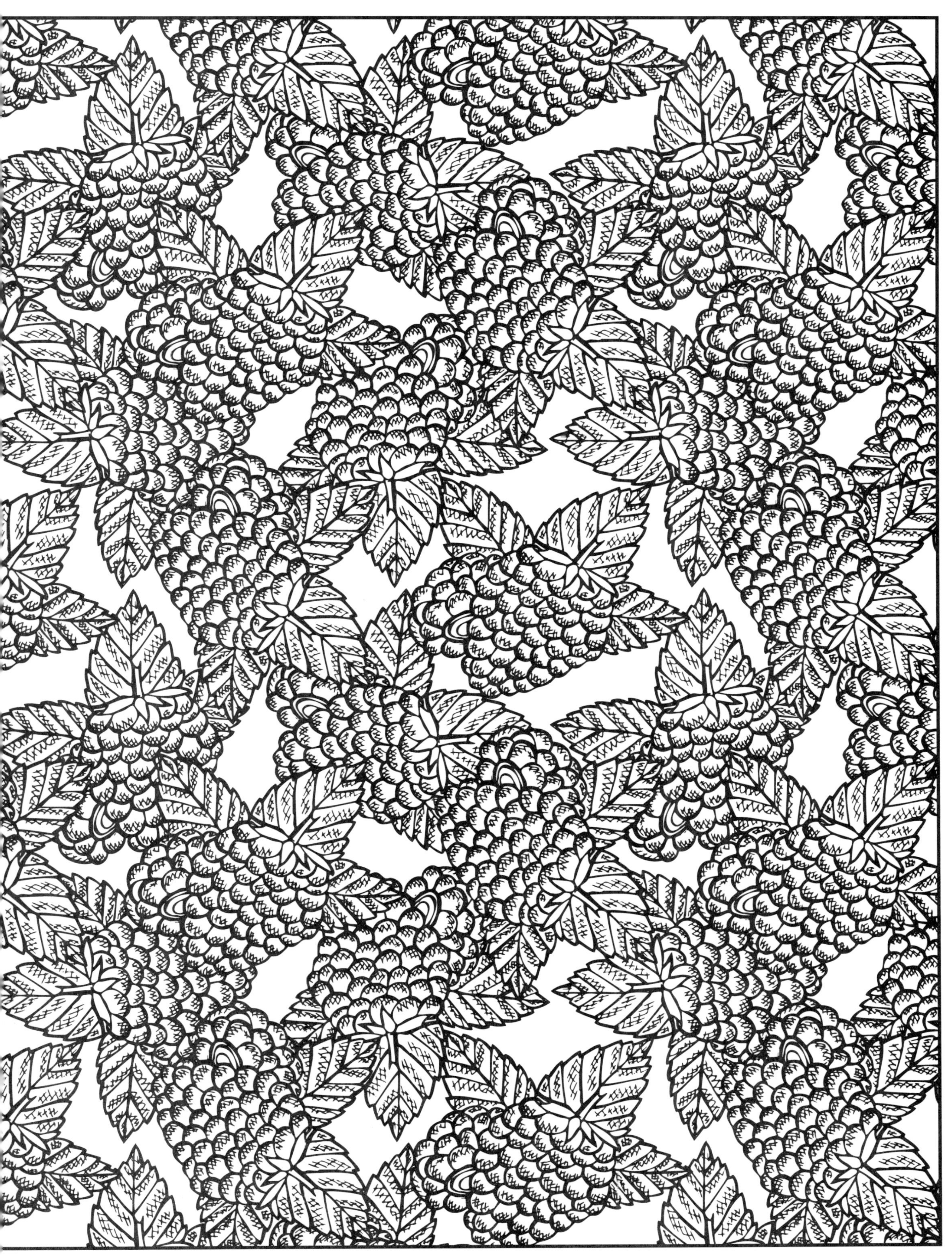

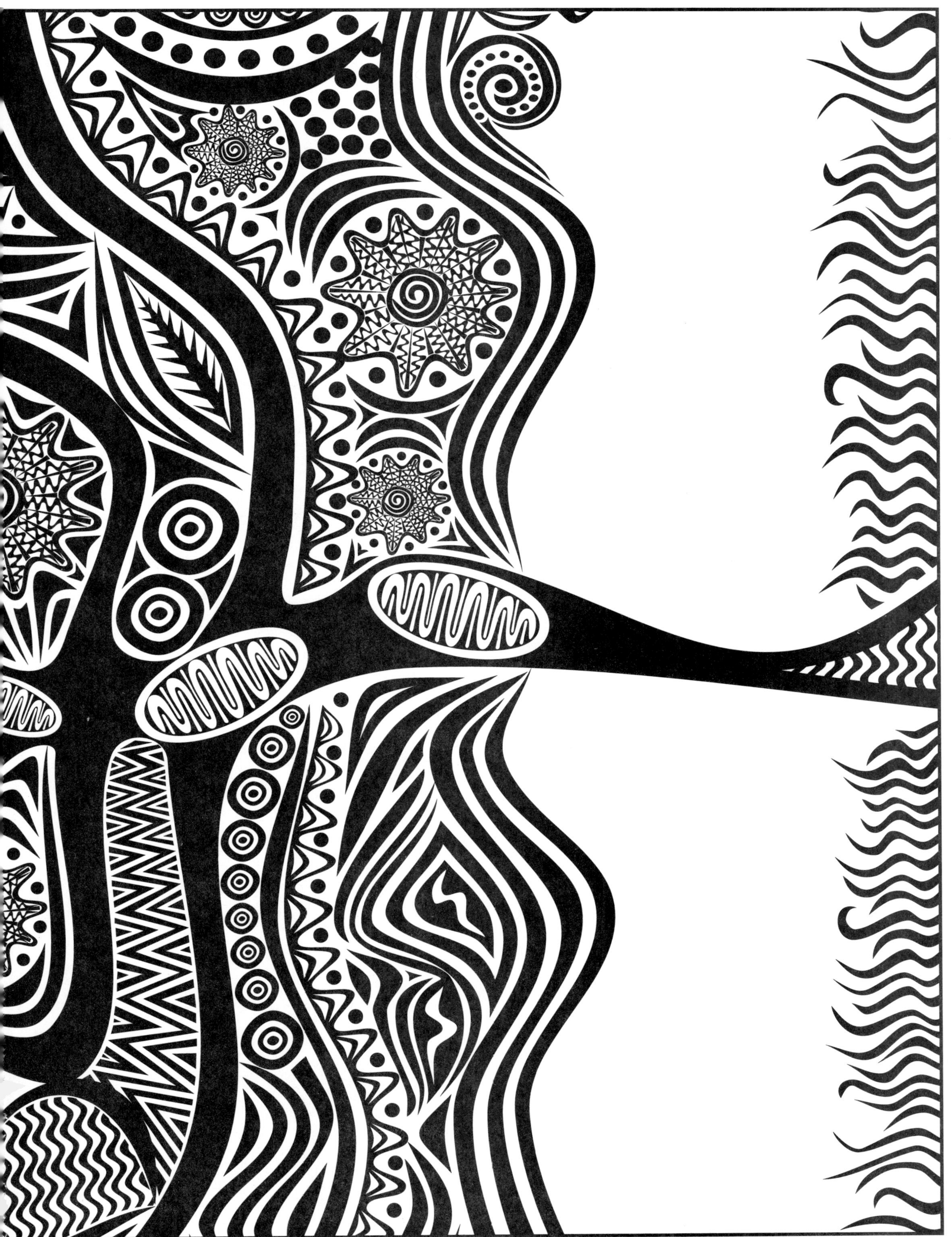

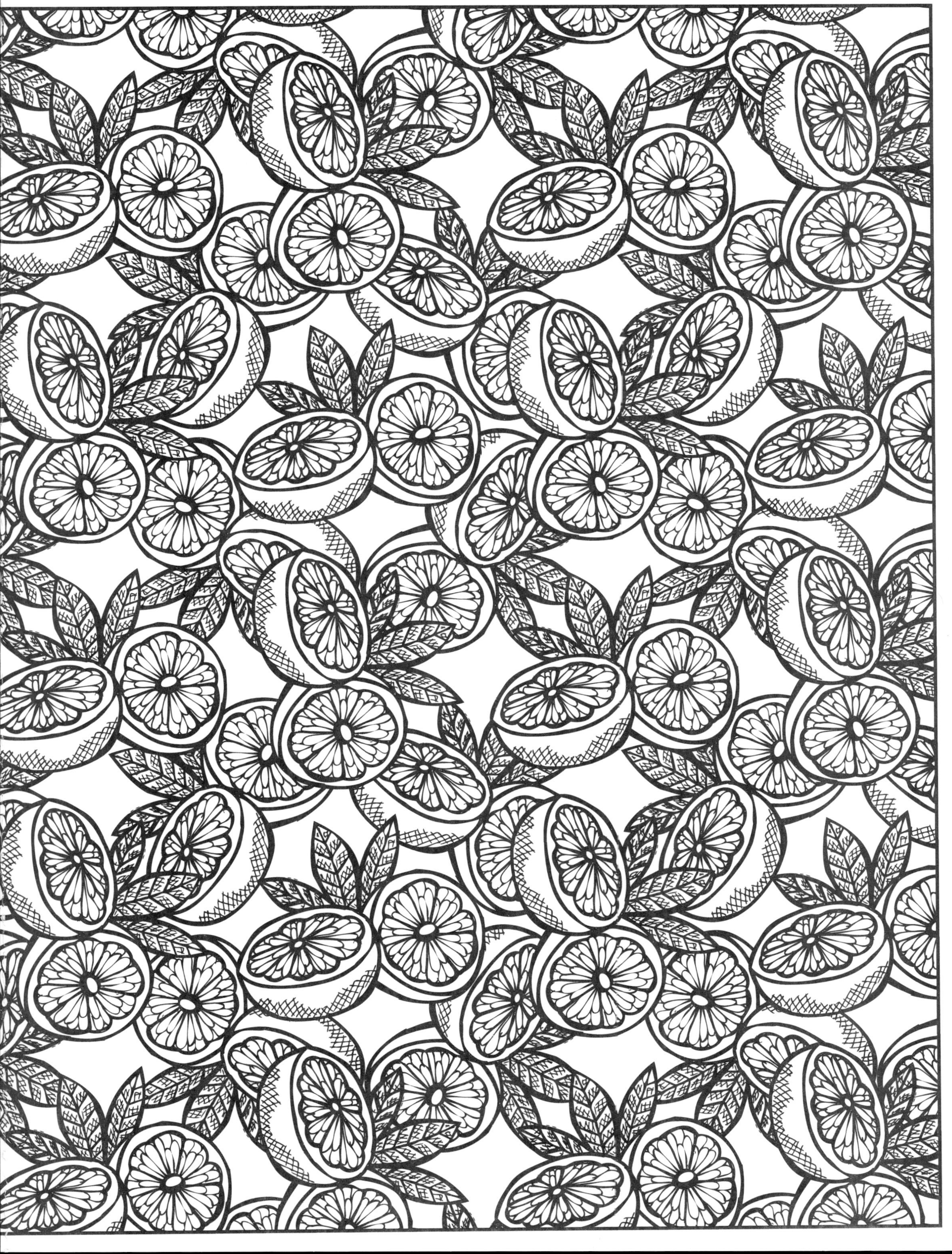

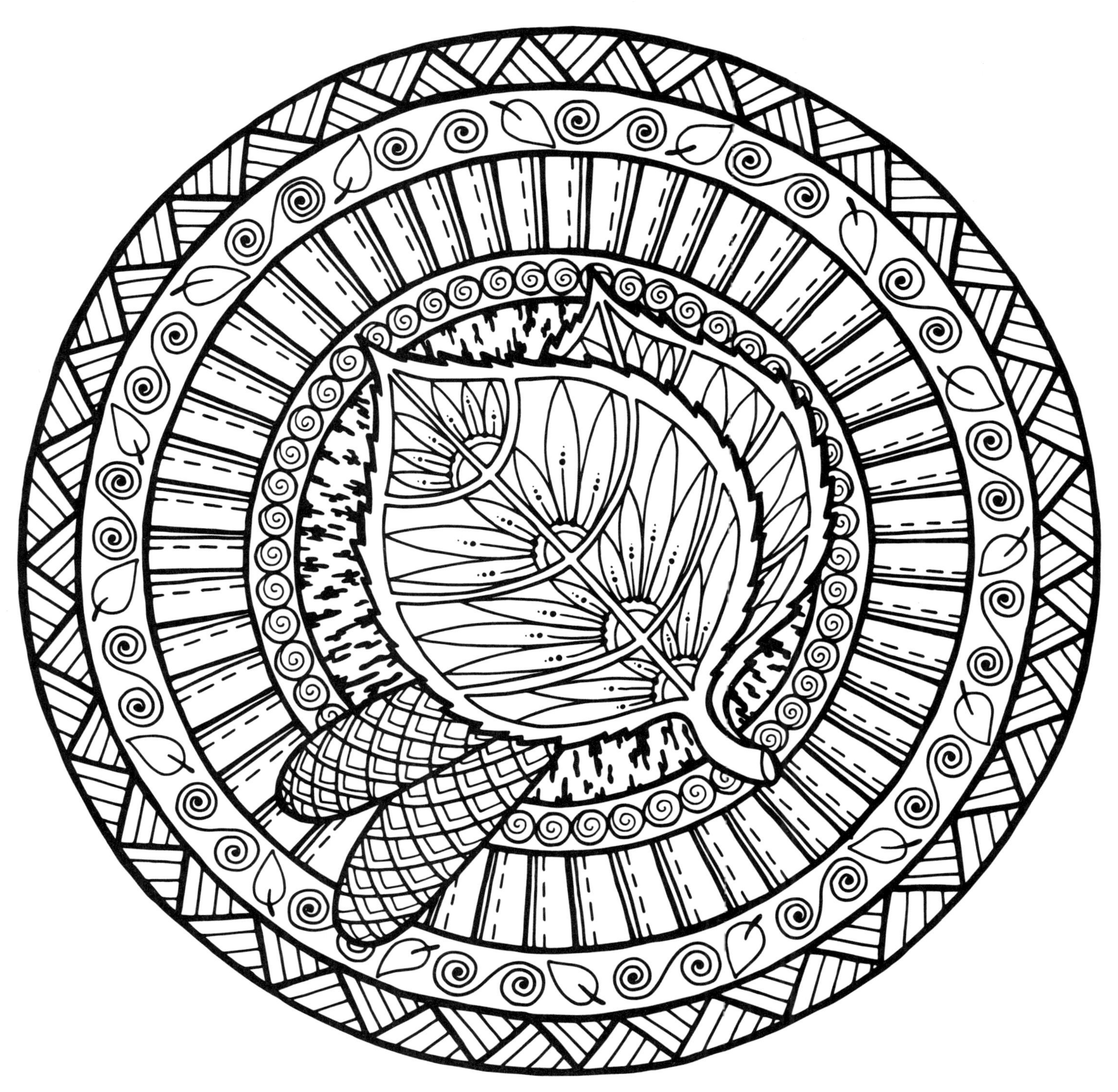

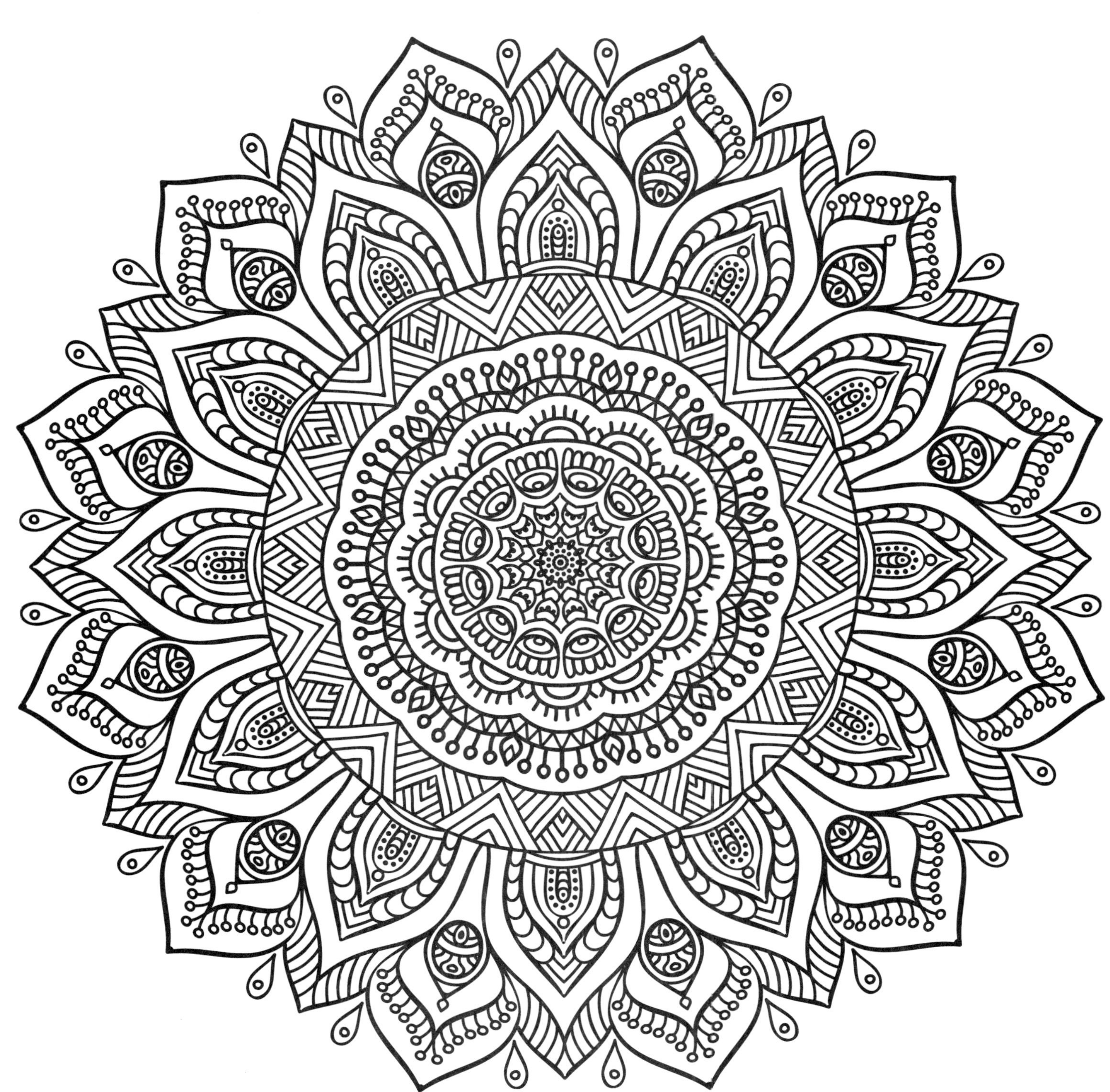

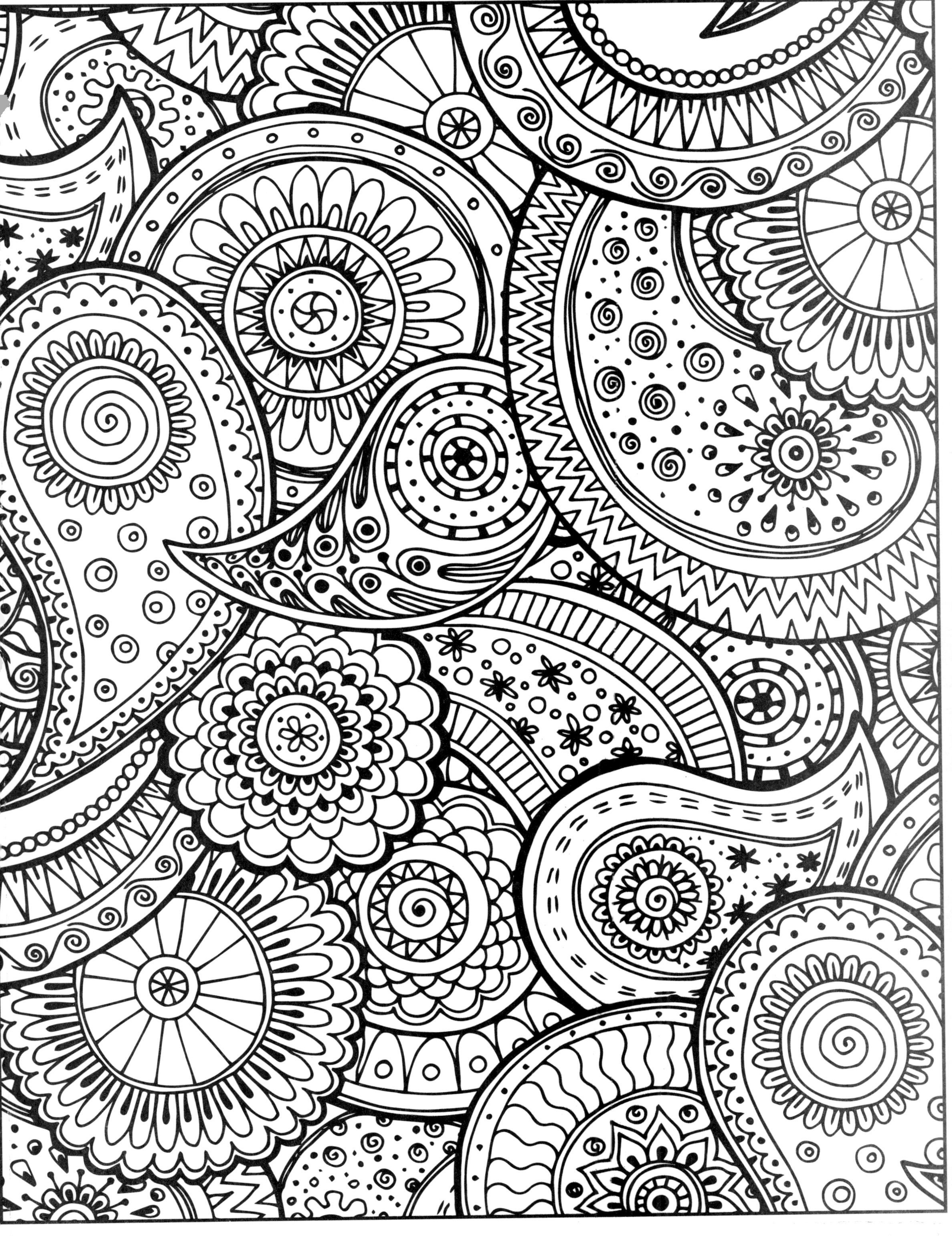

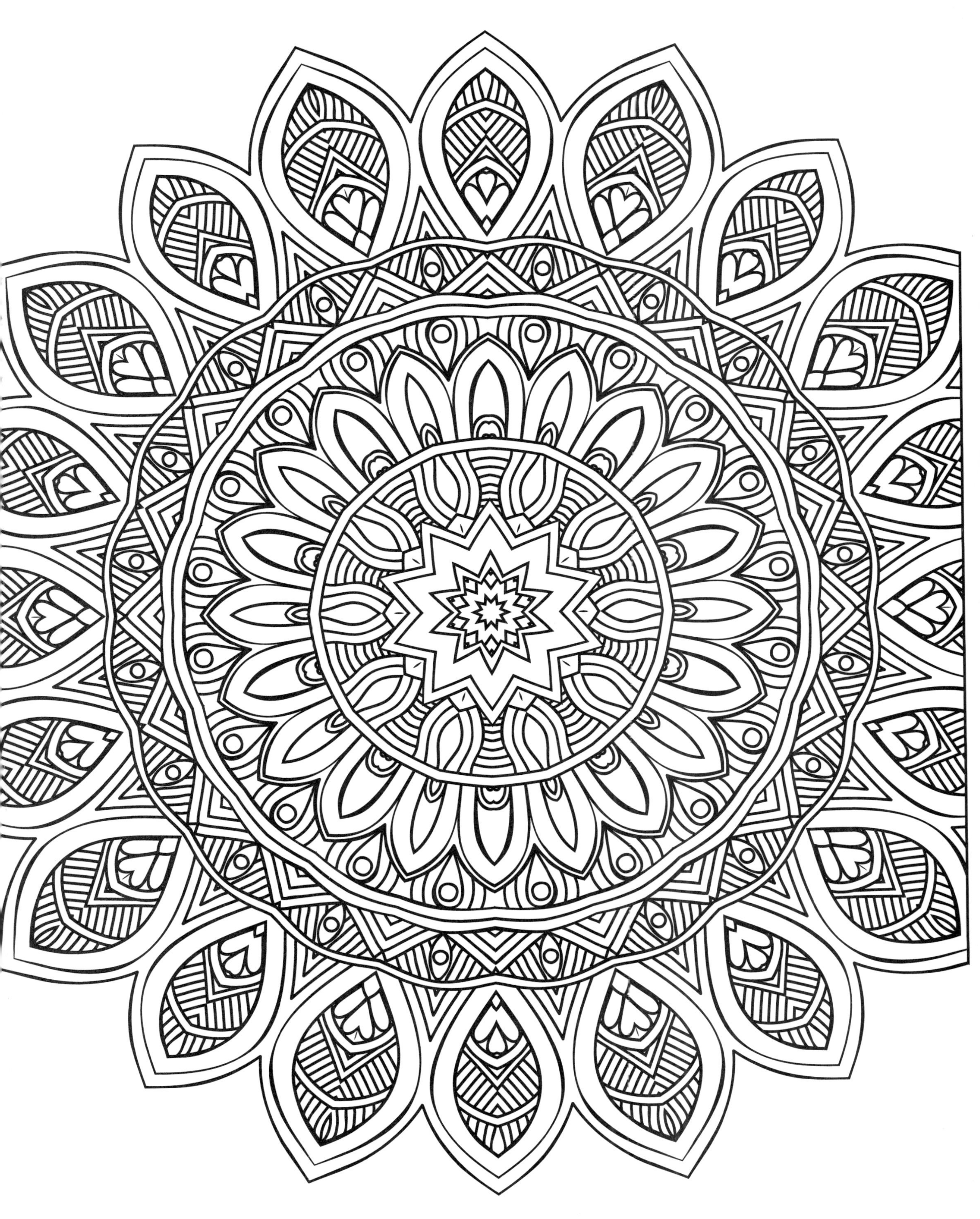

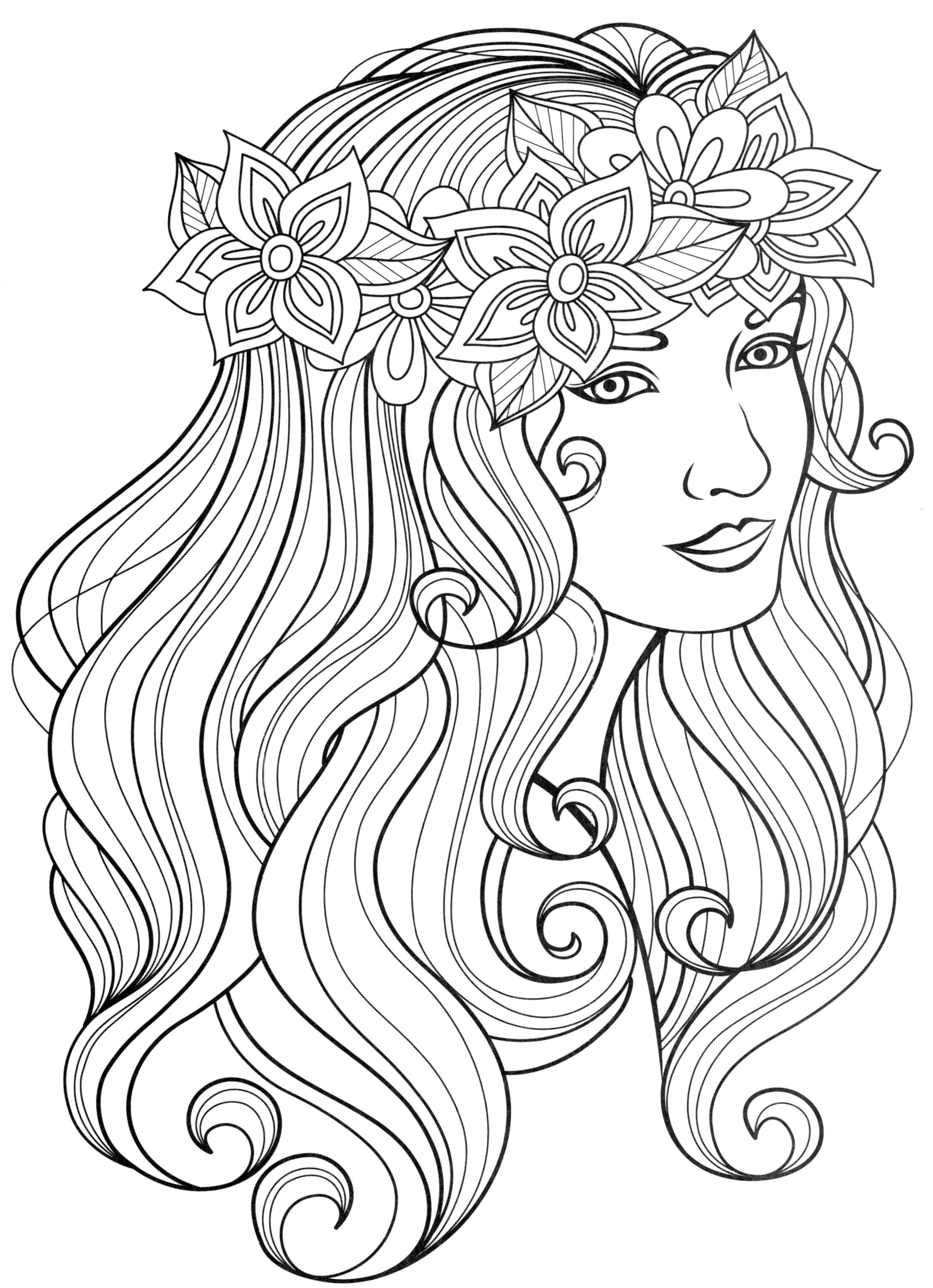

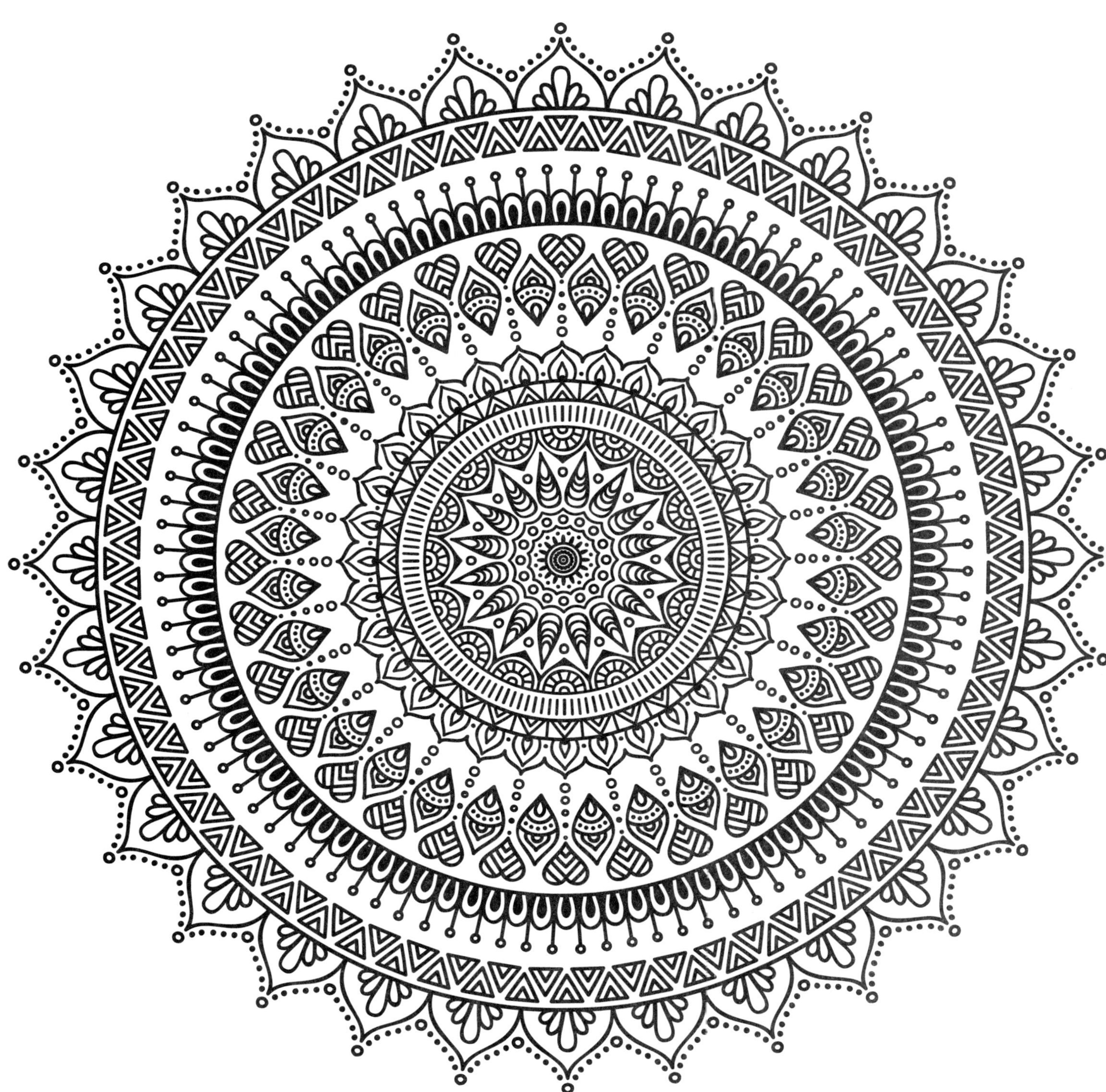

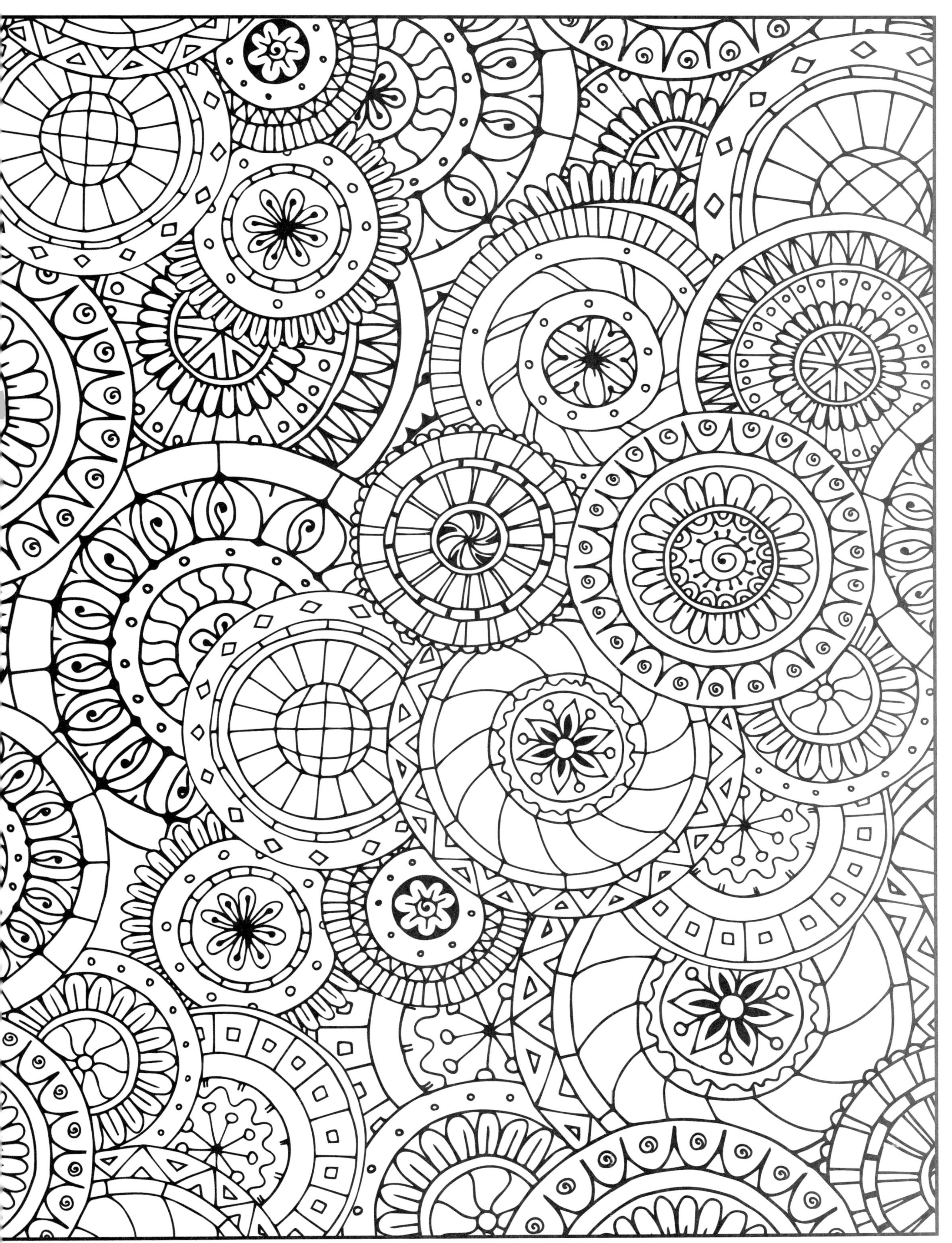

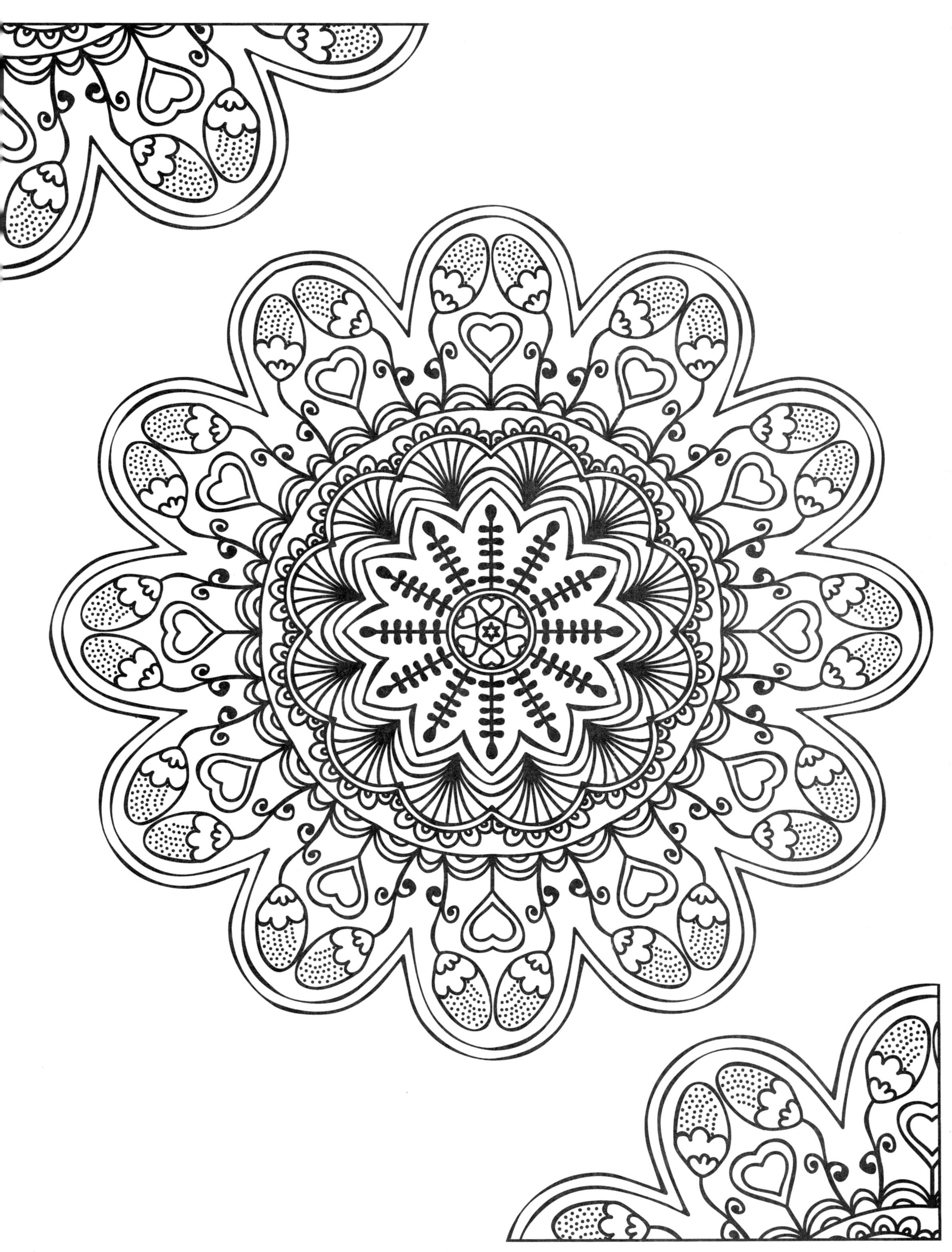

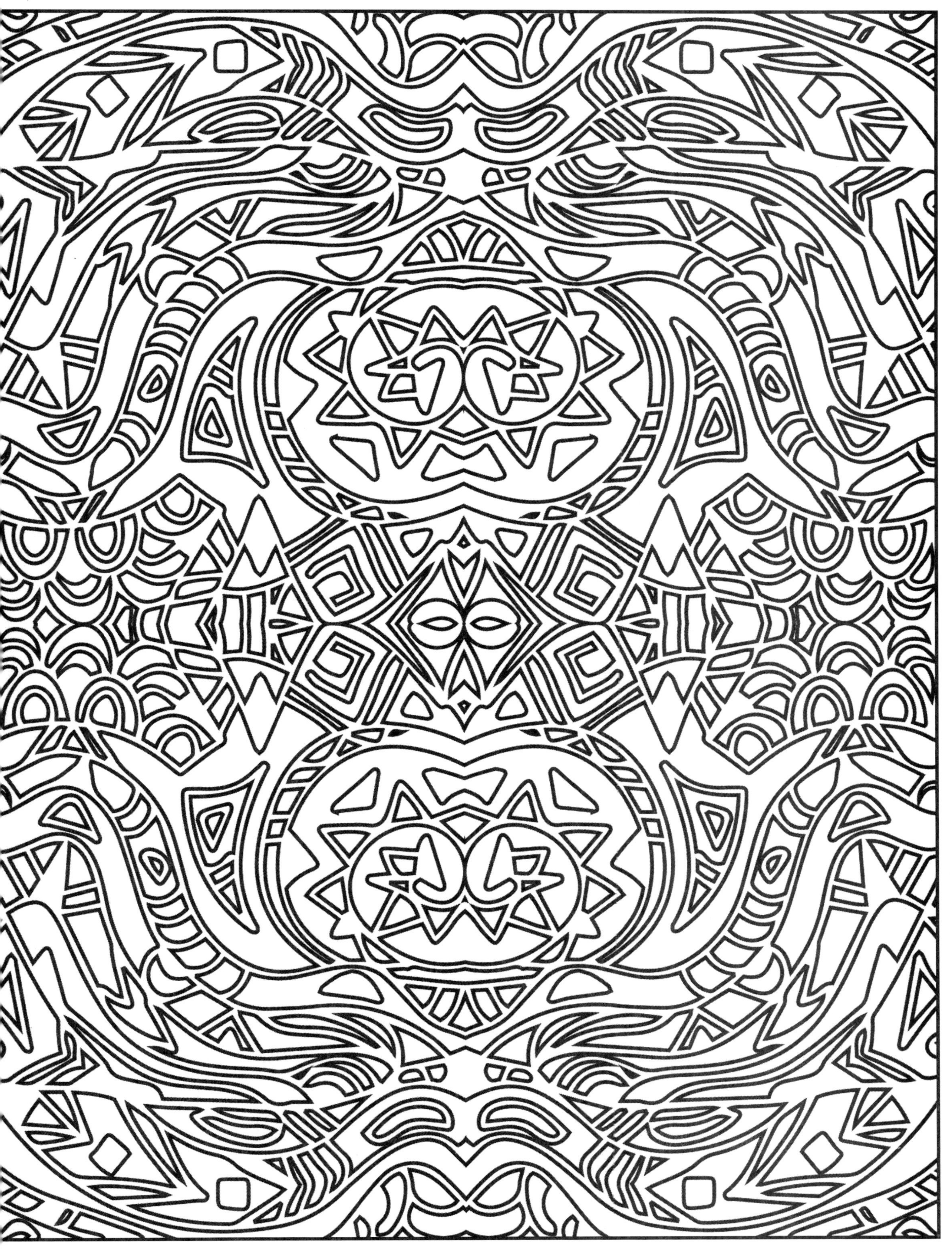

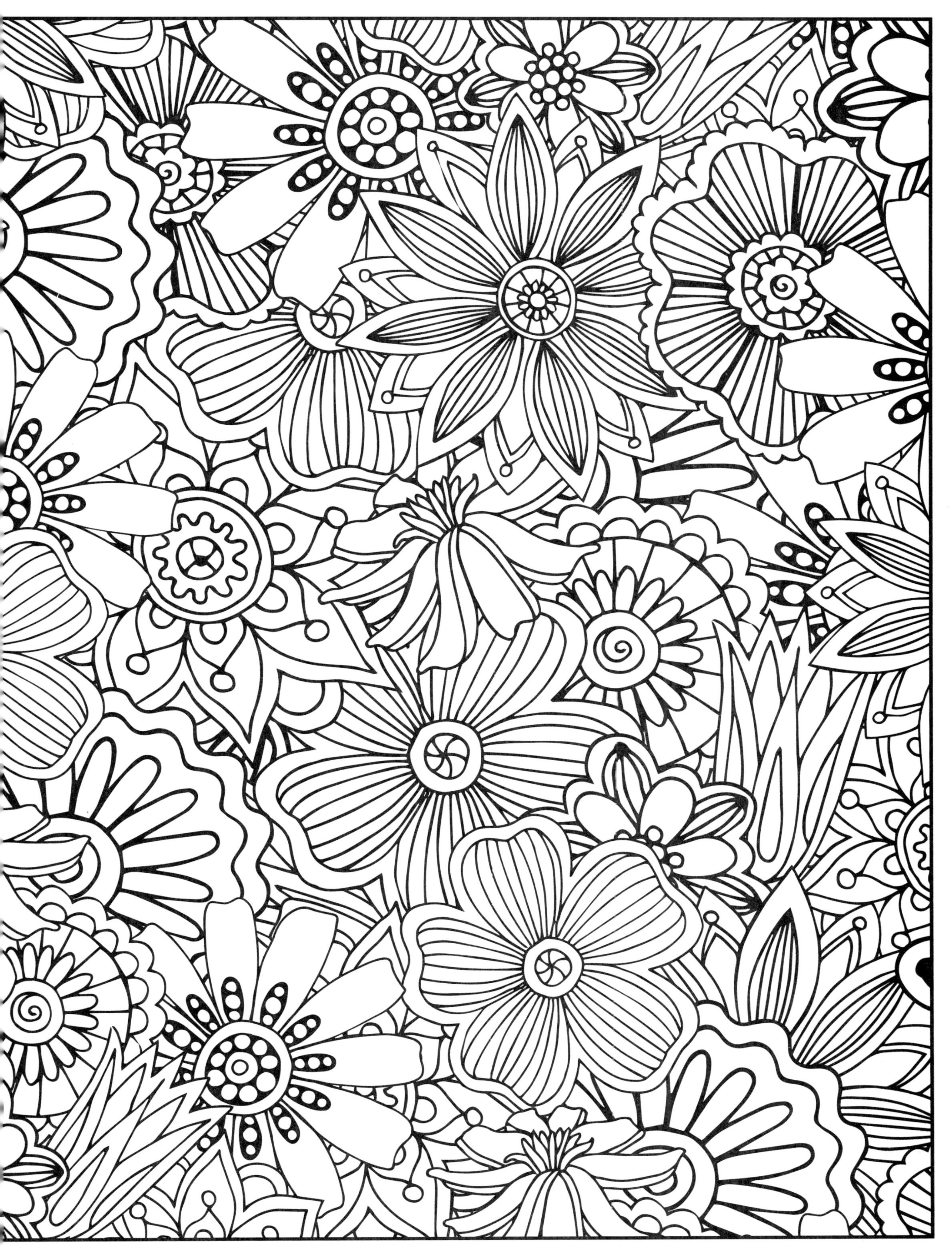

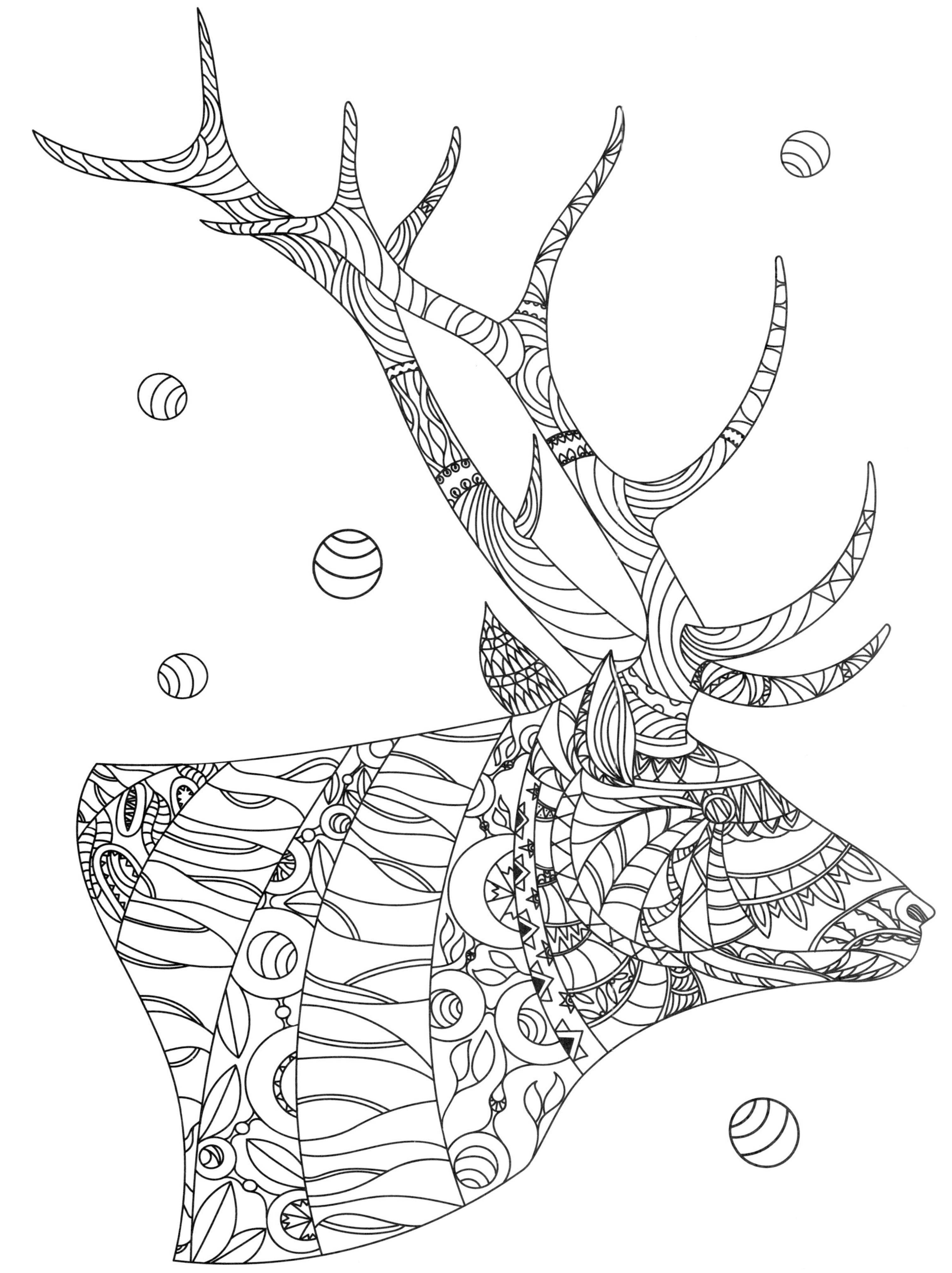

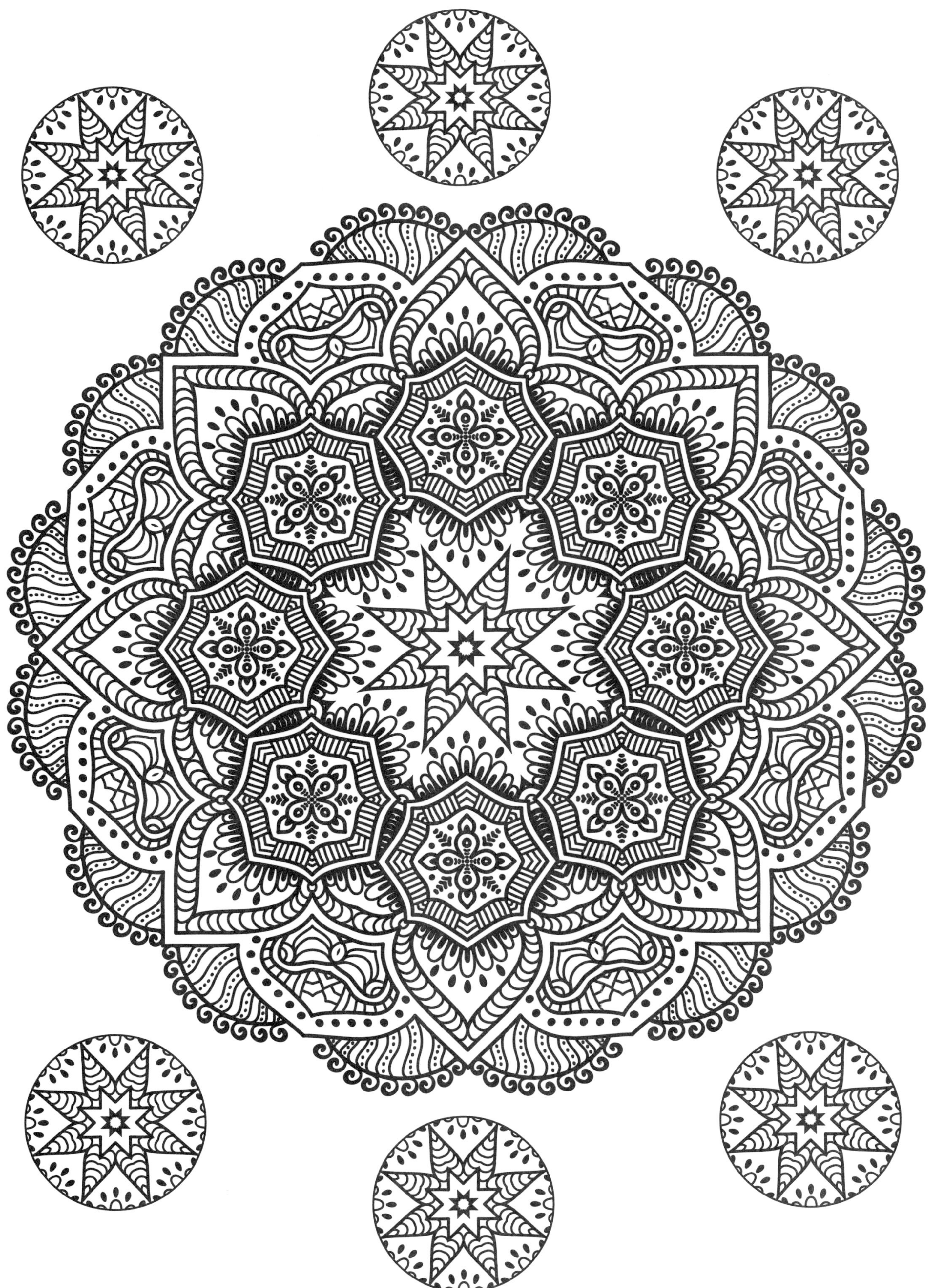

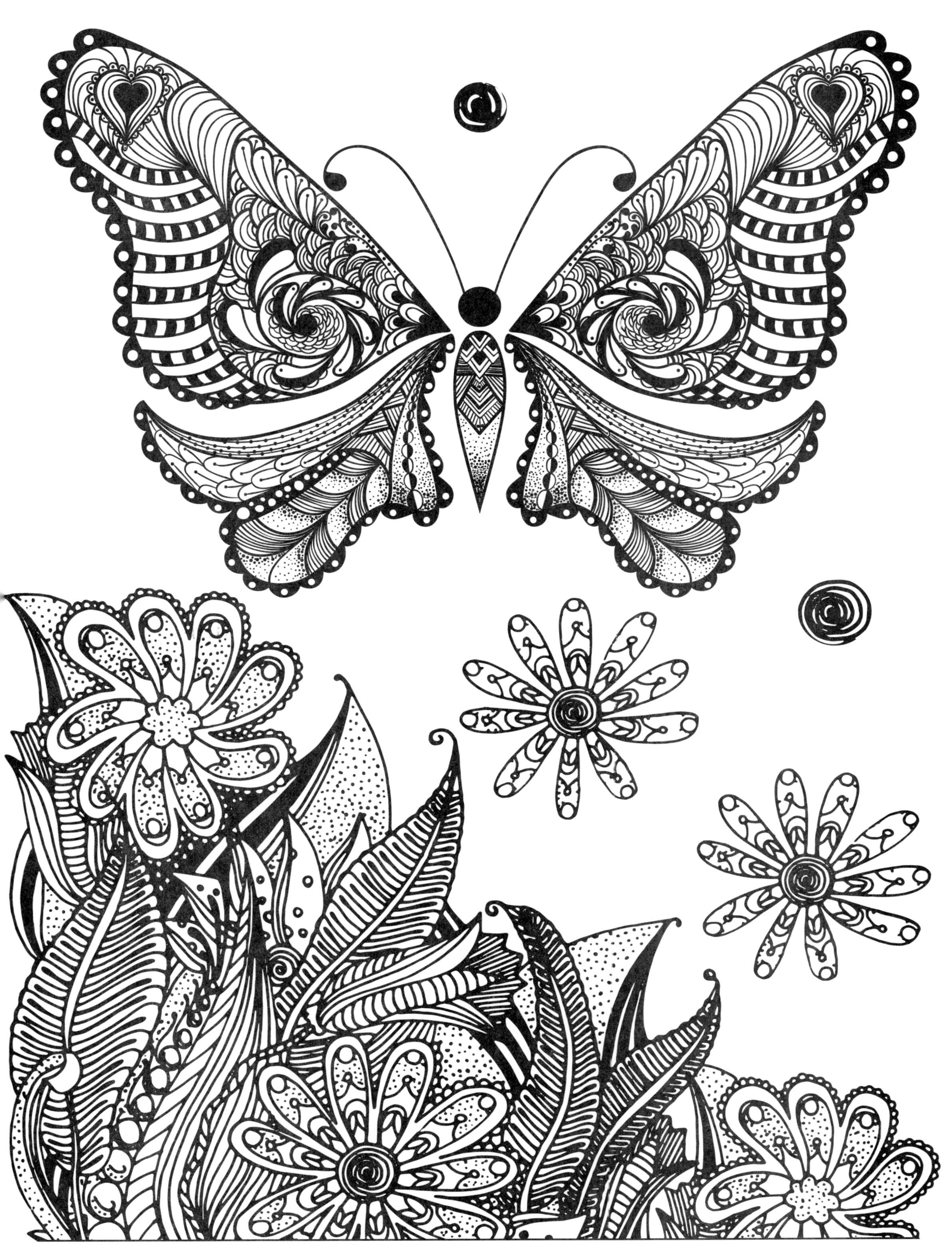

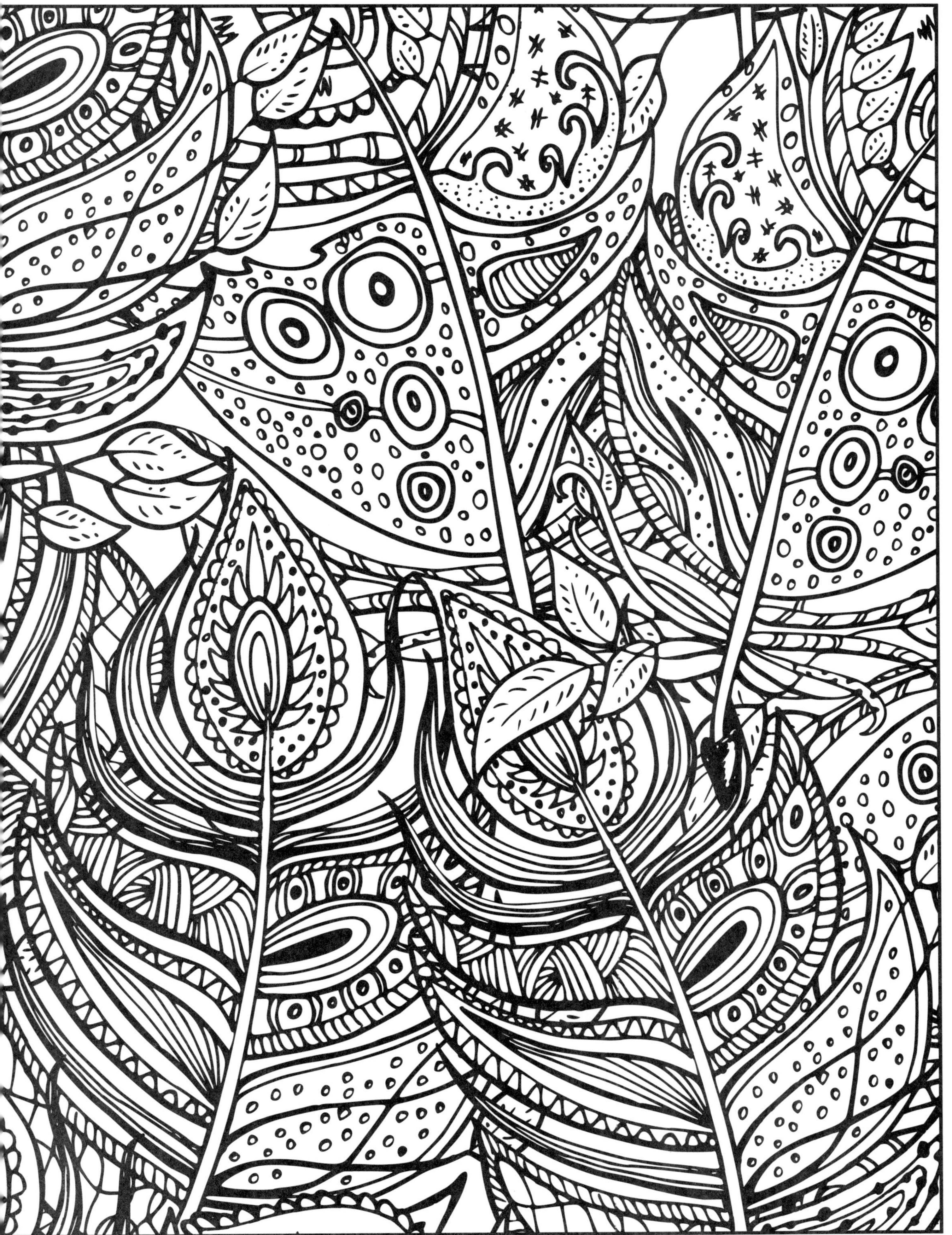

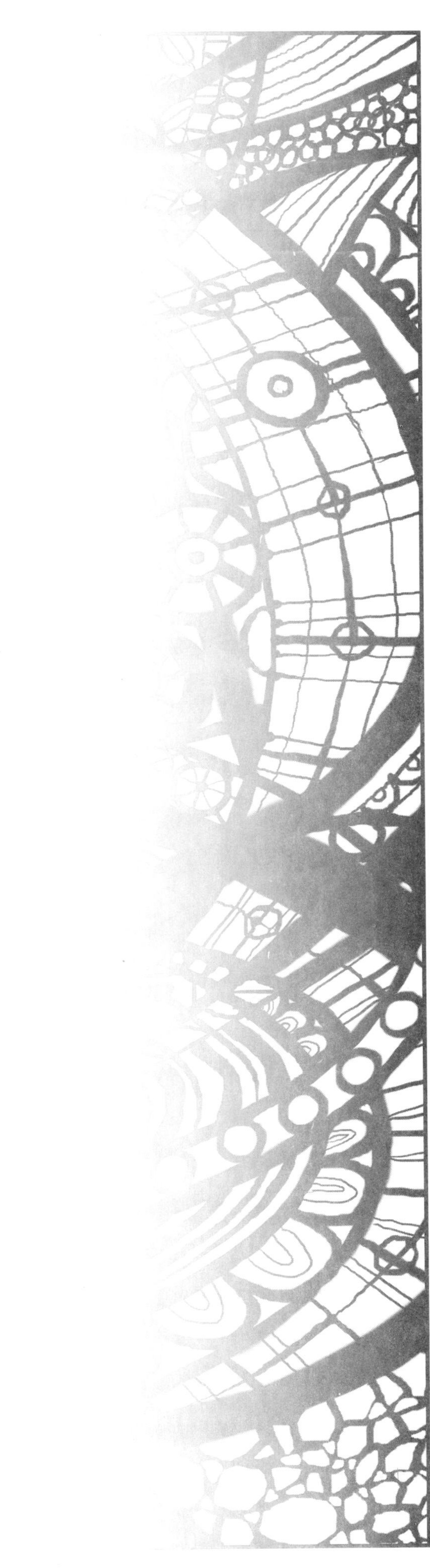

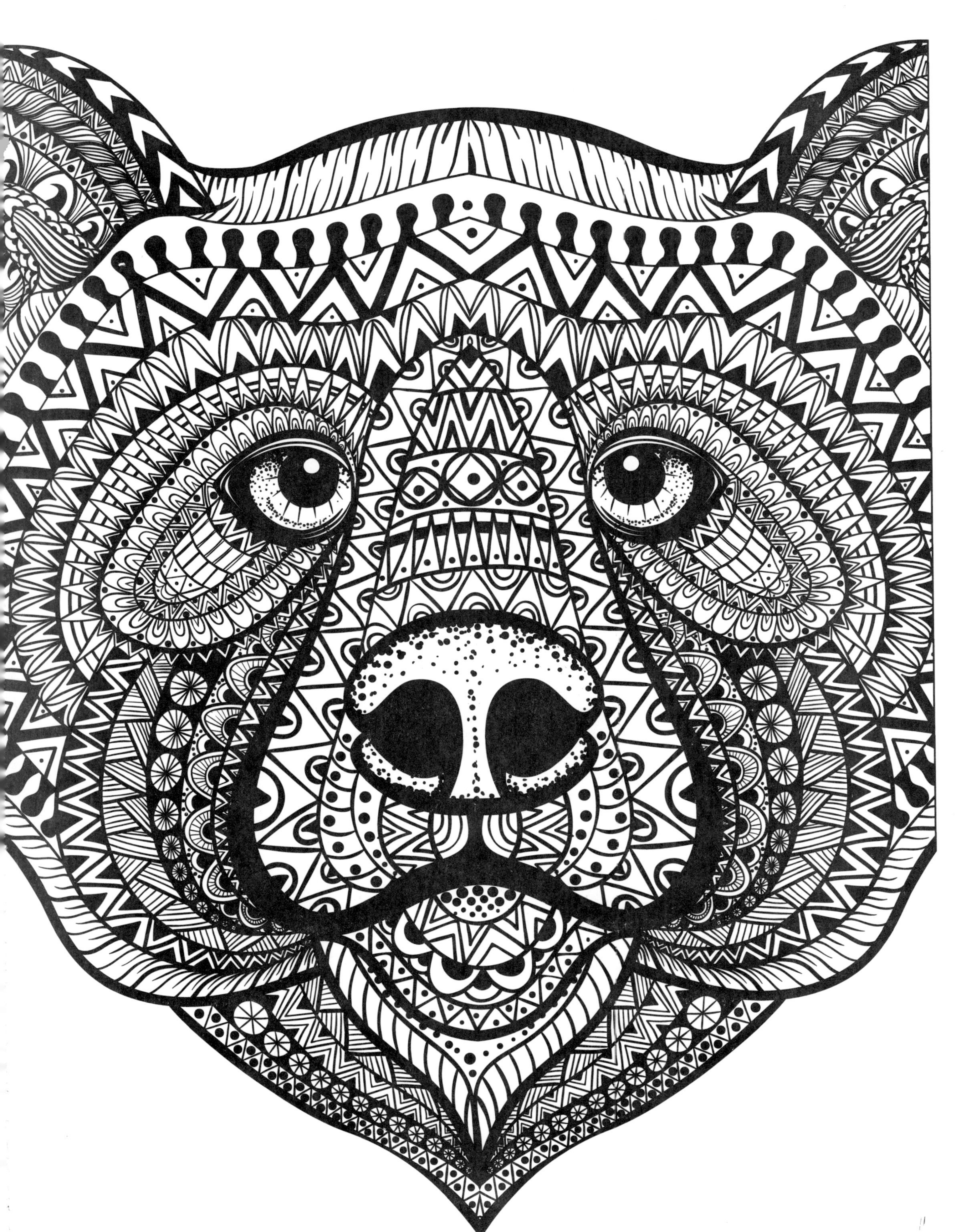

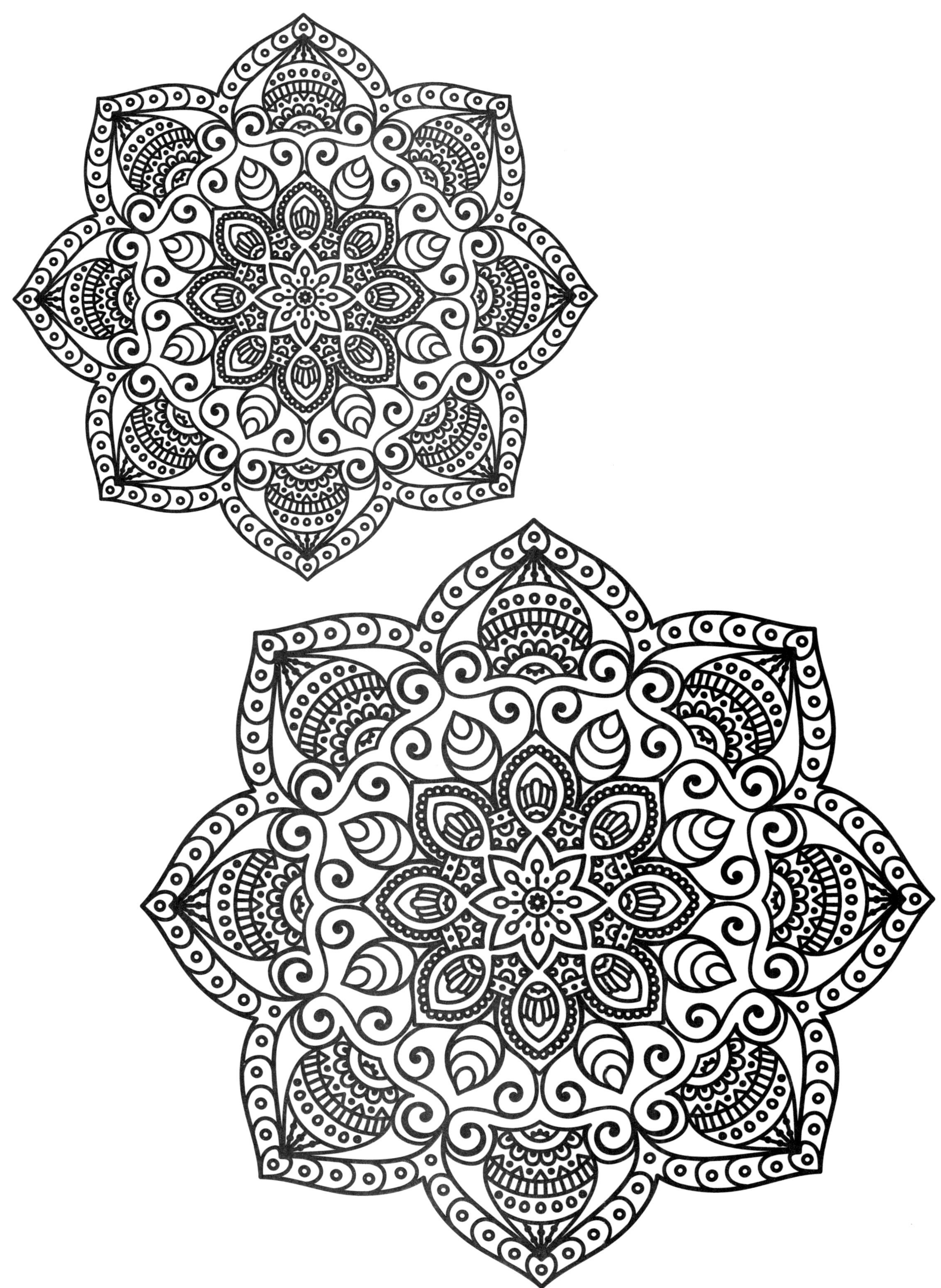

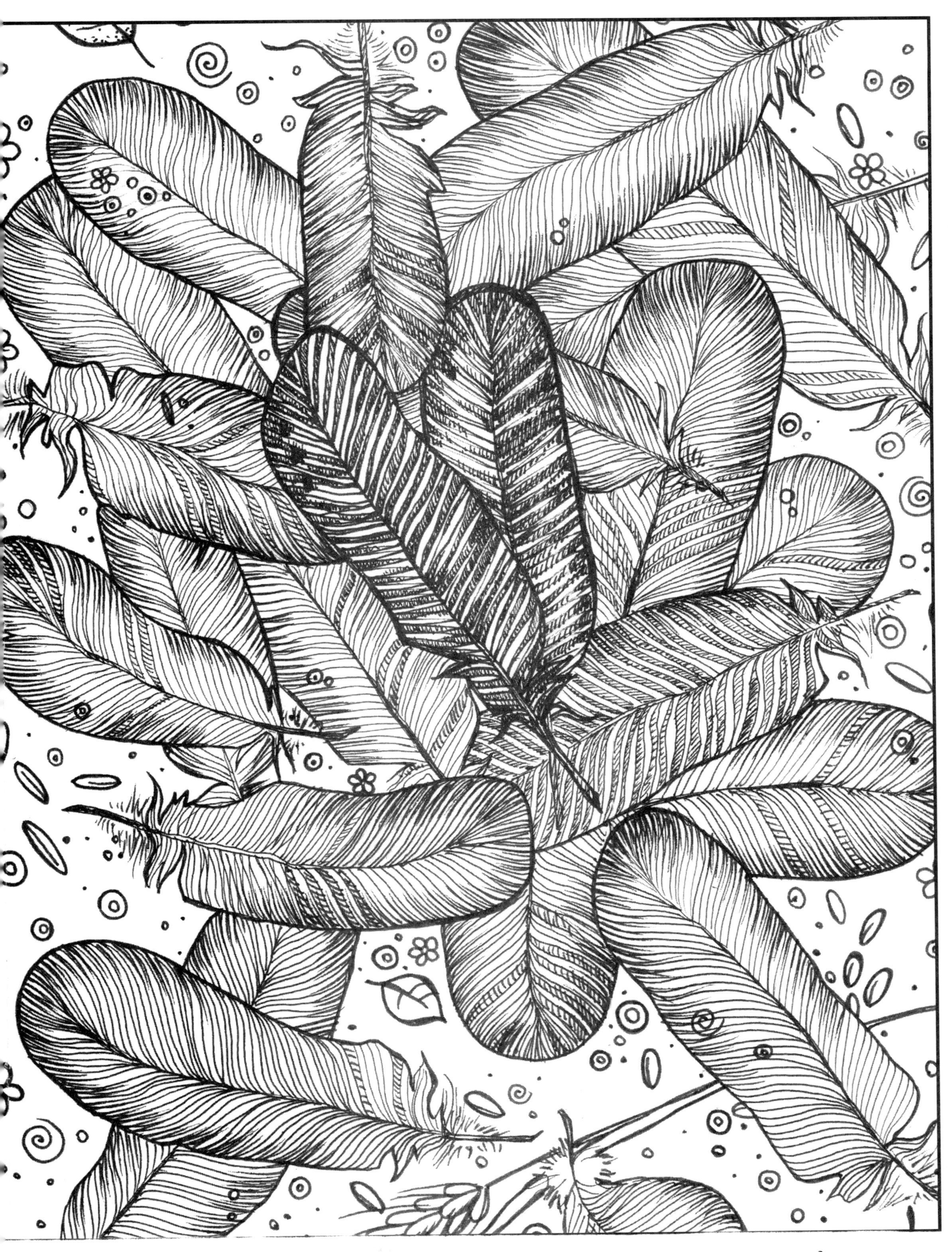

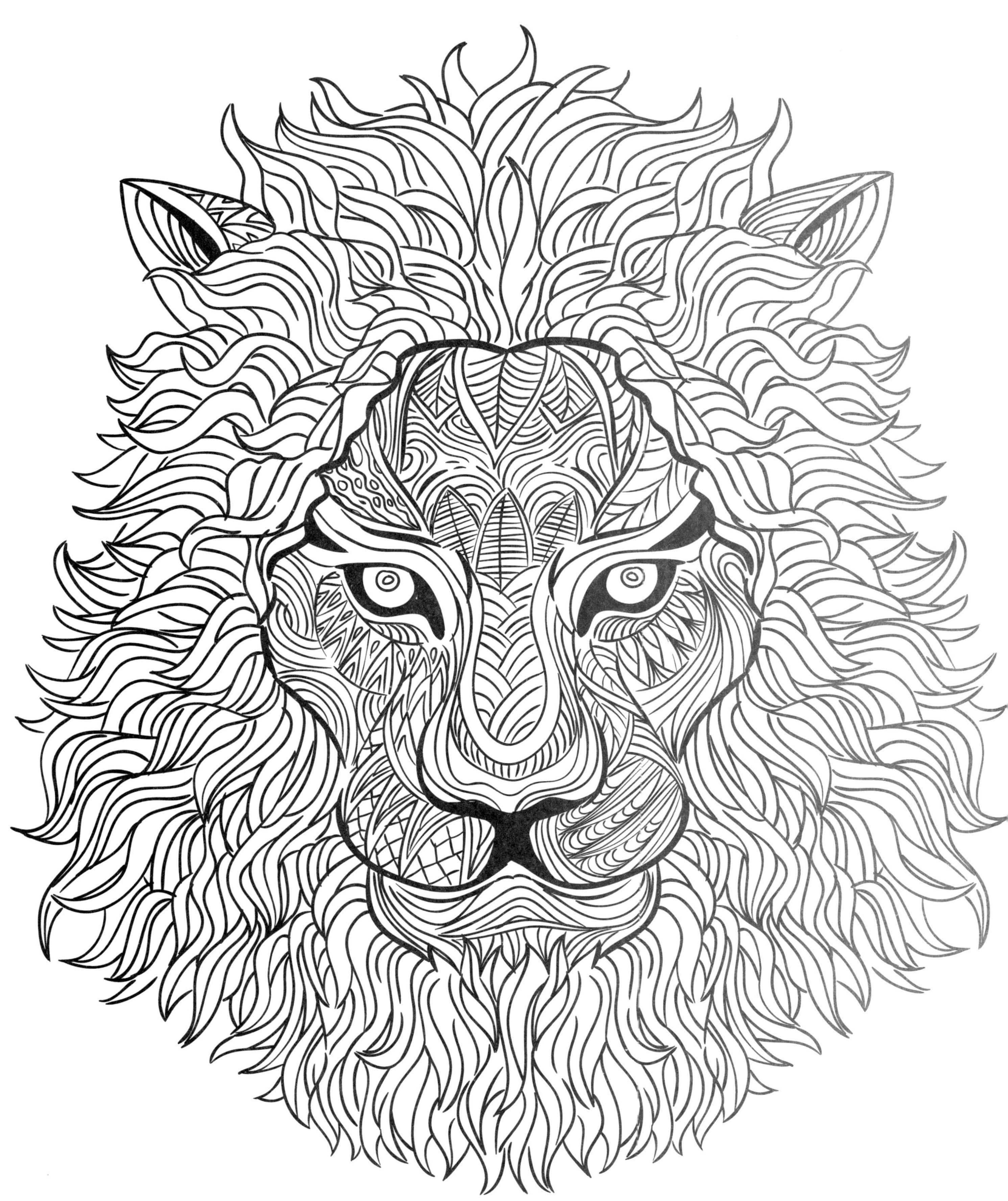

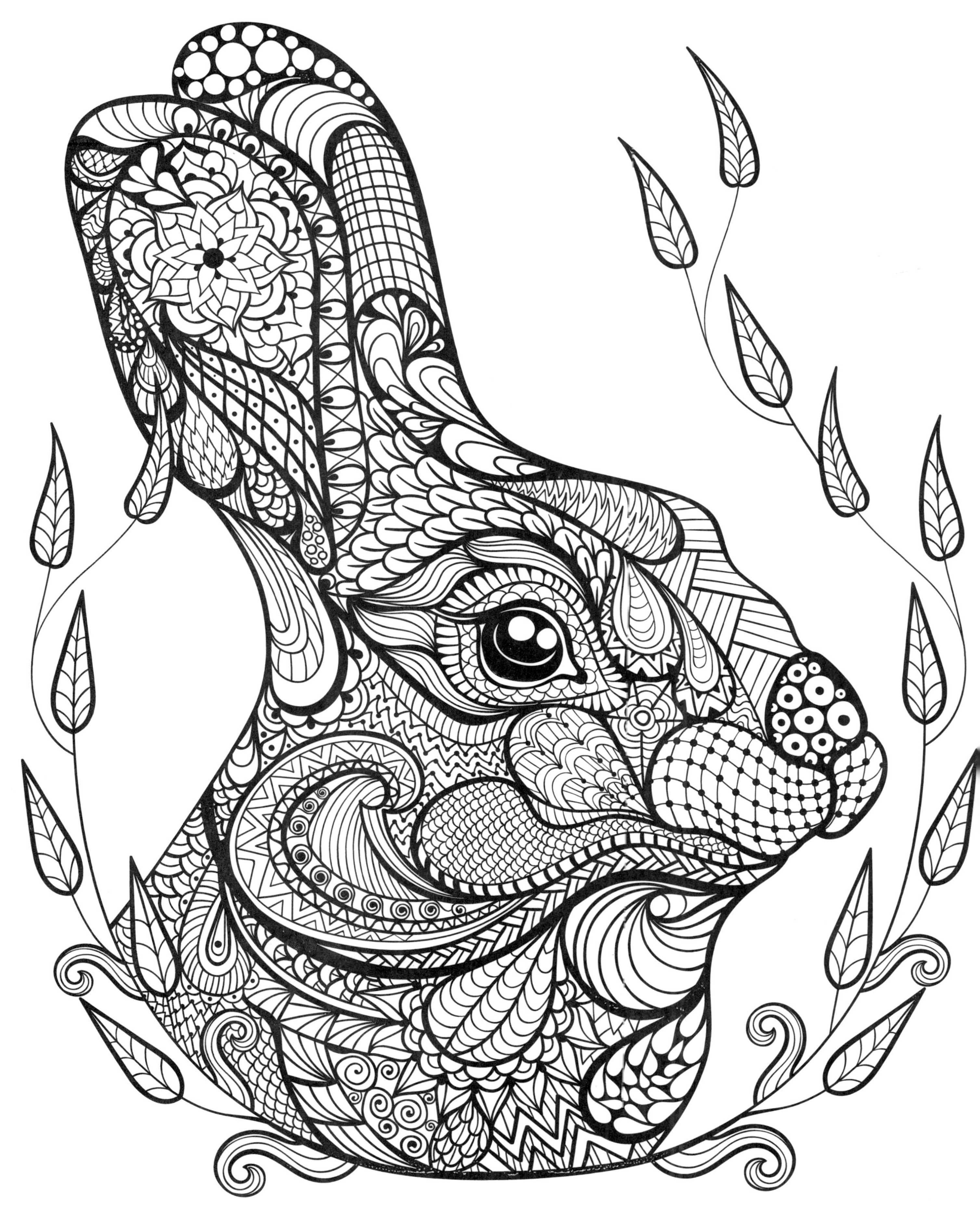

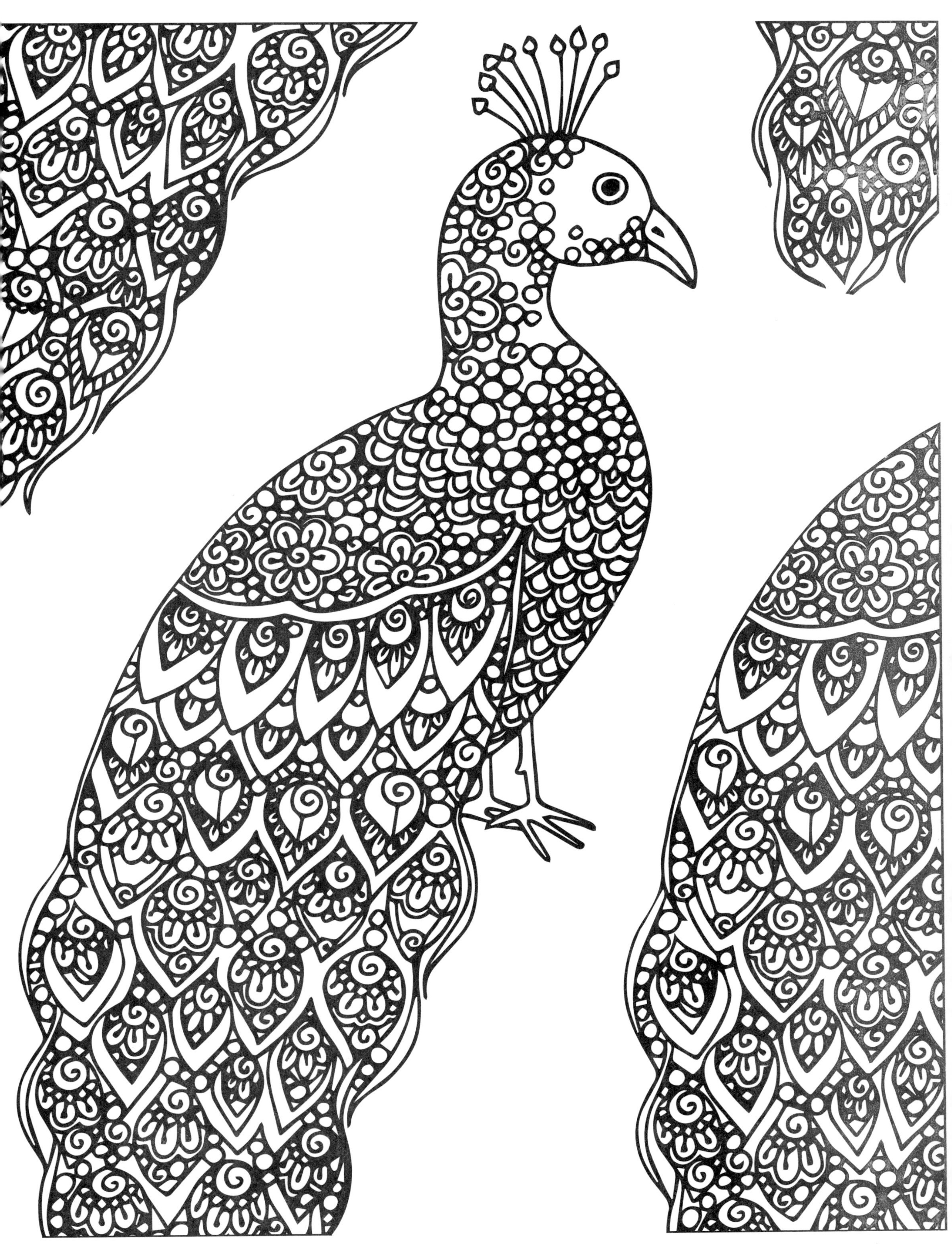

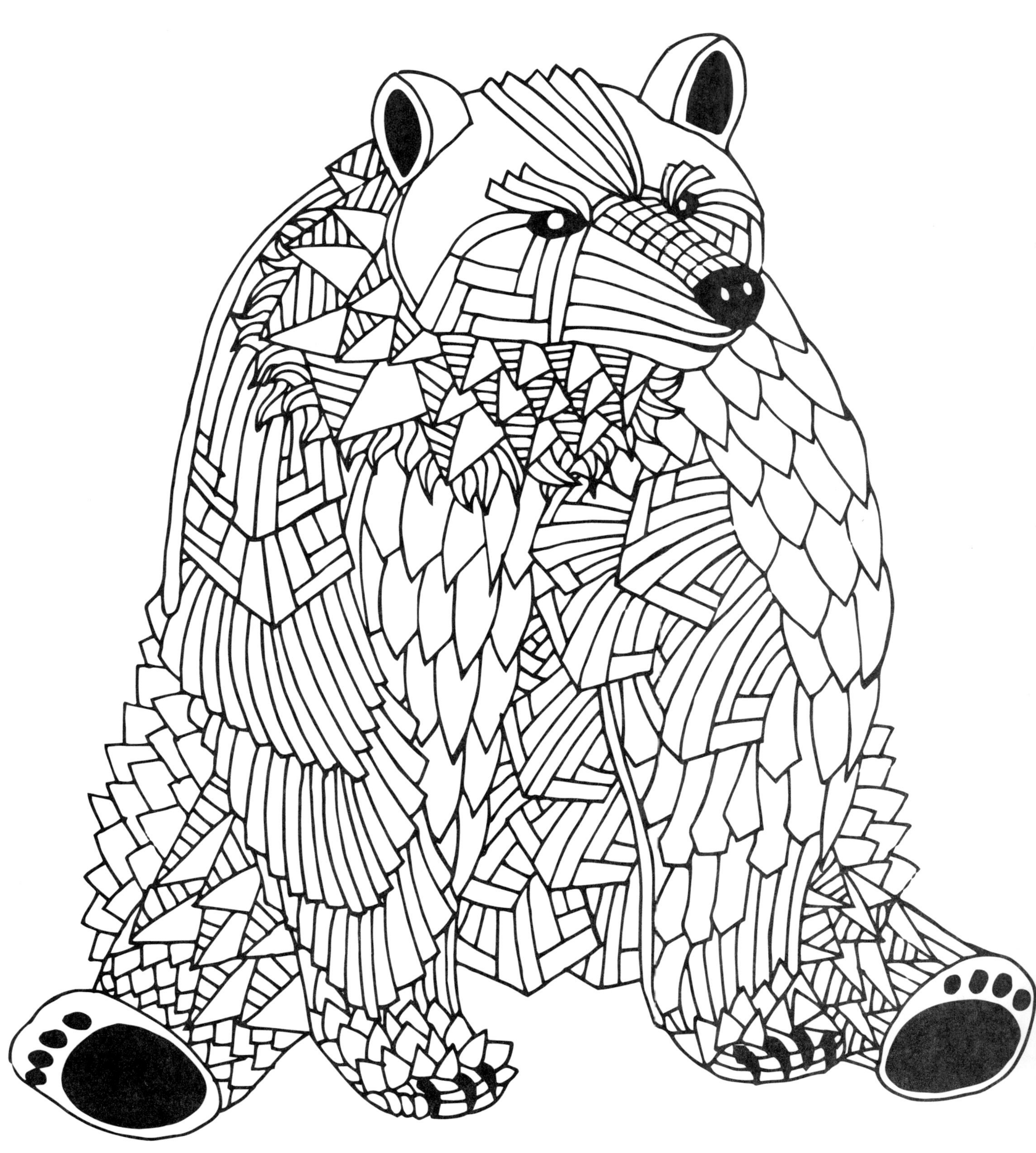

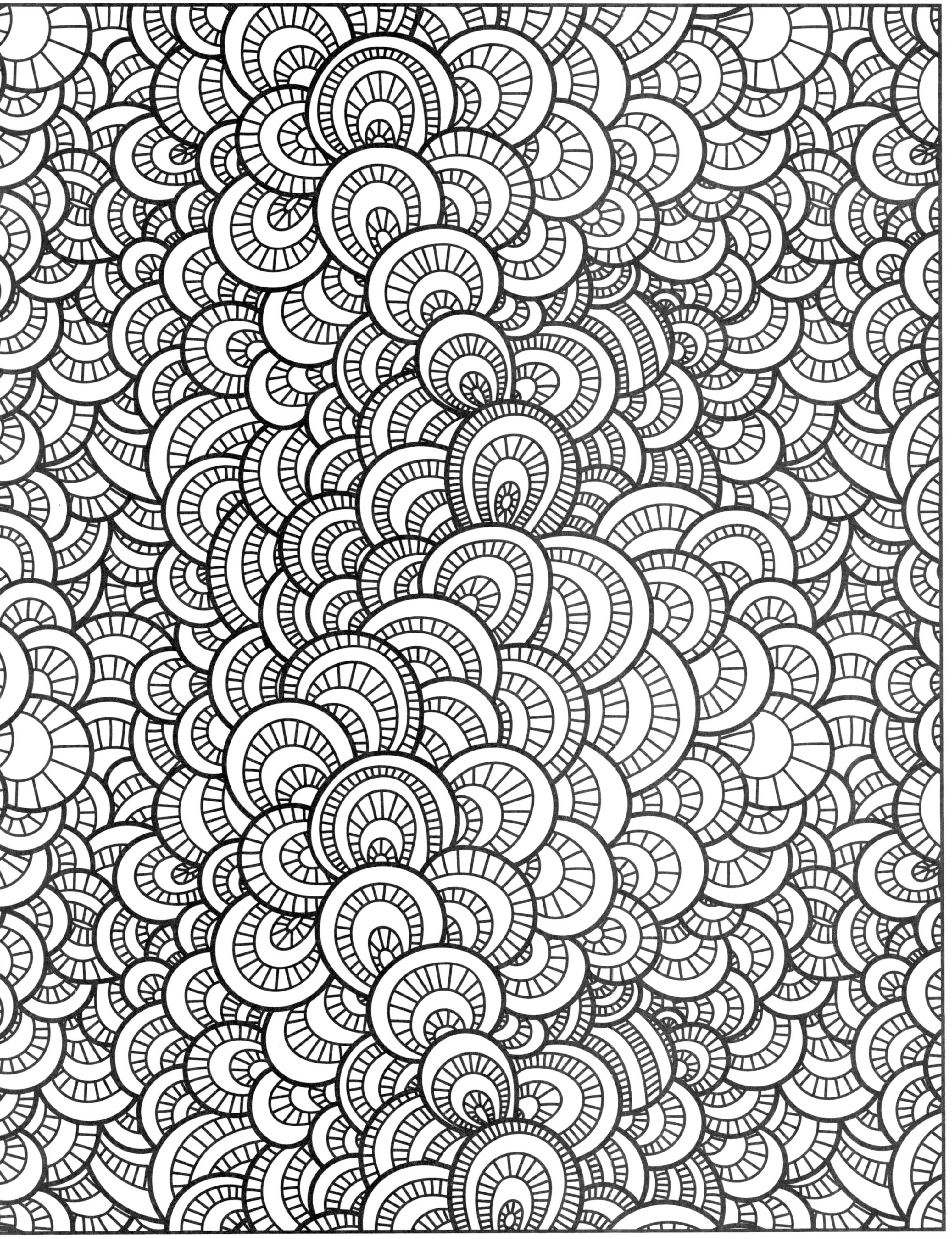

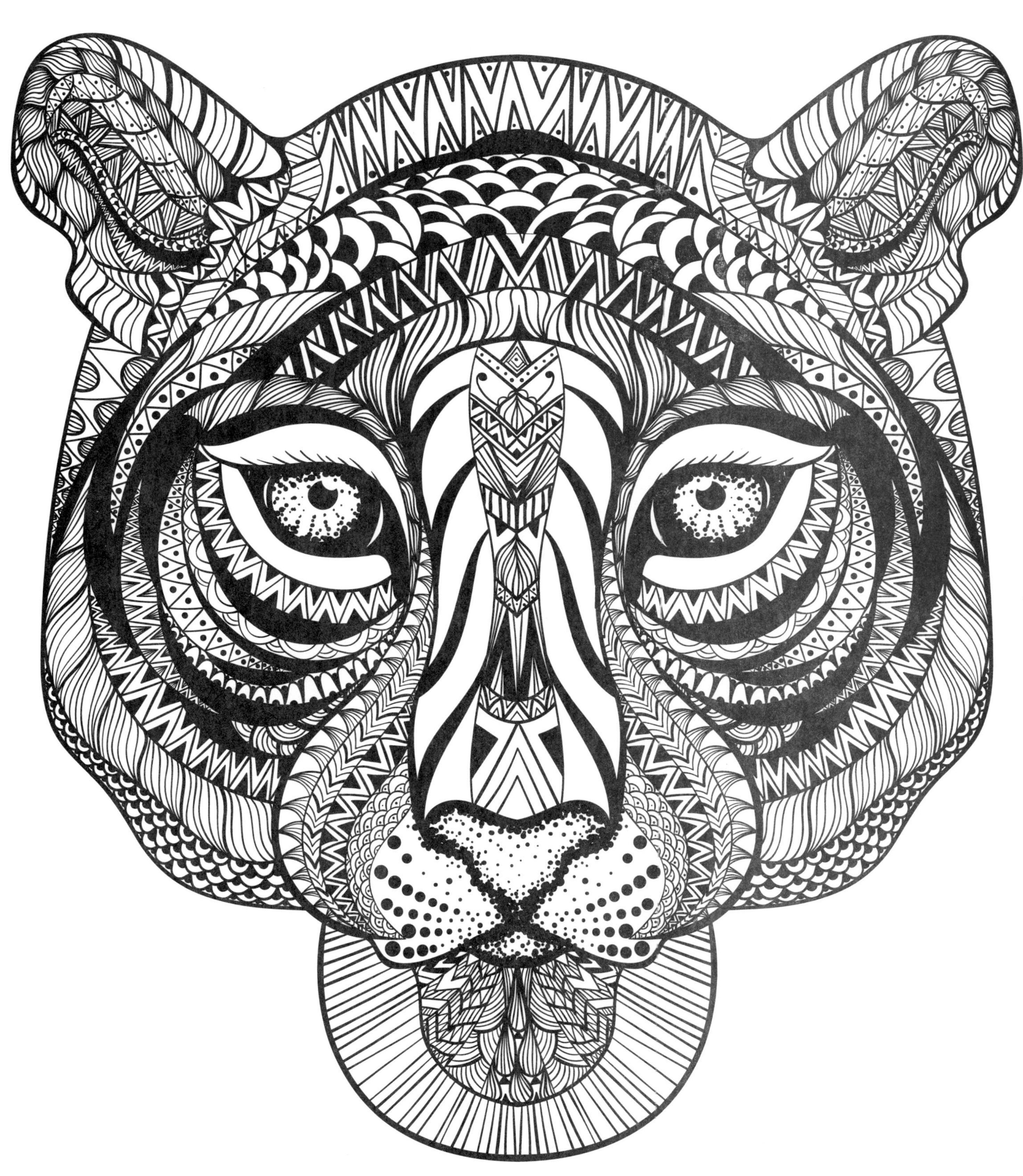

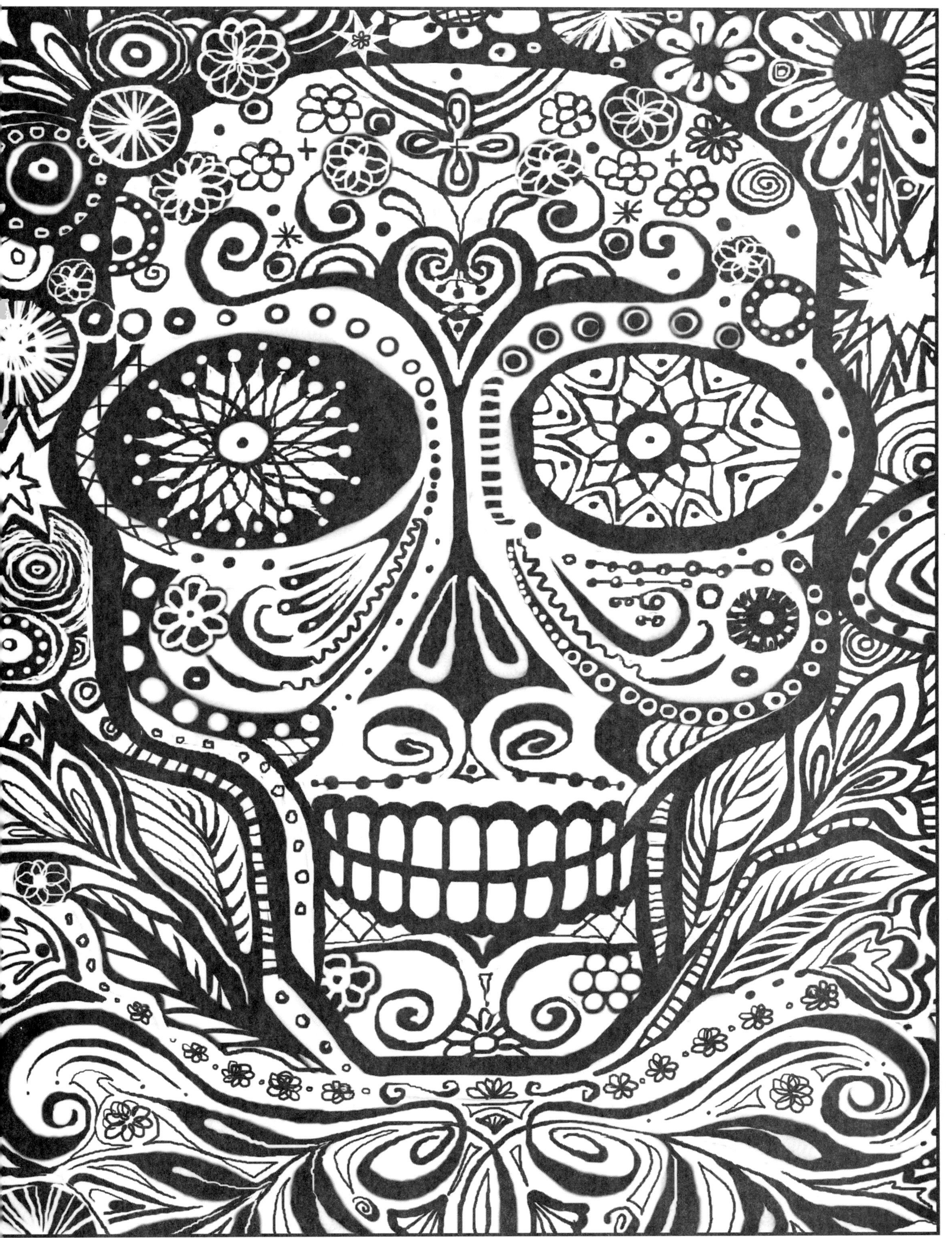